A HOLLYWOOD NEWSHAWK MYSTERY #1

The CITY BURNS at Night

ROGER ALFORD

THE CITY BURNS AT NIGHT
© 2019 Roger Alford

No portion of this publication may be reproduced or transmitted, in any form or by any means, without the express written permission of the copyright holder. Names, characters, places, and incidents featured in this publication either are the product of the author's imagination or used fictiously. Any resemblance to actual persons (living, dead, undead, or even mostly dead), events, institutions, or locales, without satiric intent, is coincidental.

Published by Black Hood Press
An imprint of Lightning Bug Press
5535 Robinhood Village Drive, #103
Winston-Salem, NC 27106

www.blackhoodpress.com

First Print Edition: August 2019
ISBN-10: 0-9672822-0-9
ISBN-13: 978-0-9672822-0-6

Printed in the United States of America

10 9 8 7 6 5 4 3 2 1

DANGEROUS DALLIANCE

IT WAS dark when I made it back to my apartment stash. The only lights were from the street lamps, doorways, and scattered windows here and there. I'd just parked my bucket when one light in particular grabbed my attention. It was right across the street and the brightest of all.

Don't know how I hadn't noticed it before. But there it was in all its blazing glory. Right there on the marquis of that old movie house across from my hovel.

IRENE FAYE in
THE WOMAN IN QUESTION

The picture was about a fellow named Johnny. Down on his luck and drinking his way through Mexico. He gets a job working at a club run by Nick, a hot-tempered American gangster. The only kind.

Enter Irene. She played the gangster's moll, Laurel. A luscious blonde with smoldering eyes and curves in all the right places. Naturally, the poor sap falls for her. And falls hard.

In person, Irene was really something. I'd already gotten a taste of that. But seeing her there, up on that big screen, in all her glory? Well that was something else.

I could see where any guy would fall for her. Head over heels. She'd still be there in his grey matter long after the lights went up. And then he'd dream about her night after night when he got home.

She was a siren. A goddess. The kind of dame that drives a fellow bonkers.

The kind of dame that a fella would kill for.

ALSO BY THE AUTHOR

THE BLACK SPECTRE
Ghosts in the Asylum (Book I)
No Victory Without Scars (Book II)
Vengeance Waits at the Door (Book III)

Invitation to Death
and Other Thrilling Mysteries (Volume I)
Death is a Silent Intruder
and Other Thrilling Mysteries (Volume II)

HOLLYWOOD NEWSHAWK
The City Burns at Night
Dreams Die at Sunset (Extra)
The Red-Headed Ruse (Extra)

For a complete list of books, visit:
www.blackhoodpress.com/all-books

CHAPTER ONE

SOON AS I hit the second floor of the apartment inferno, I was sure I'd never make it out alive. I still had another floor to go and it wasn't down. It was hotter than Hellfire in there. The walls were all aflame. Pieces of burning ceiling dropped everywhere I turned.

My lungs were already full of scorching smoke. The floor looked like it would give out any minute. But there were two little tykes trapped on the top floor. And I was gonna get 'em out. Or burn alive trying.

This was my introduction to Hollywood.

Yeah, Hollywood. They call it the "City of Dreams." Most people think it's nothing but glamour and glitz. That's why hundreds of young kids come out here every day, hoping *their* dreams will carry them to the top.

A few actually make it. But most of them just end up on the bottom of the heap. Before they finally pack it up and head back home. Back to the real world.

Yeah, I came out here, too. Right after the war. But I'm a reporter. I got to see the rotten underbelly post haste. The dirt that they always try to sweep under the rug.

I learned my lesson real quick, too. These days, I just watch what goes on from the outside. But back then — well, sometimes I couldn't resist the urge to get in on the act.

My big break came one night just a few weeks after I'd hit town. An apartment building downtown on Figueroa had gone up in a blaze. Like Hell had just sprung right up through the sidewalk.

I was fresh off the bus and had just dusted a chair at the *Los Angeles Chronicle*. The Dahlia case was only four months cold. Truman was halfway through his first term. And Bugsy Siegel could still sleep with one eye open.

Needless to say, I was itching for a story. The kind that would make my editor's hair stand on end. And get me a byline on the front page.

That conflagration was just the ticket I needed. Soon as I got wind of it, I saddled up my jalopy. I was down there faster than a politician on a spare nickel.

It was an old brownstone — well, old for L.A. anyways — and it had gone up like a box of matches. A bunch of rubber necks crowded the sidewalks around the trucks just to watch the inferno. It was better than anything playing at the local movie houses. And in living color, to boot.

The raincoat brigade tried whatever they could do to hose it down and get everybody out. All those people in the way gave old Chief Baker a fit of epic proportions.

Lucky me, I was in earshot.

"Get those people back behind the trucks!" he bellowed. "I don't want anyone else getting hurt if this blaze gets out of hand!"

He shook his head and cued me in on what had really put a pinch in his gasket. "What kind of *diseased mind* sets fire to an apartment building where children live?"

Arson. That was just the bit of dirt I wanted to hear. There'd been a crazy match thrower running around town torching places left and right.

No rhyme or reason to any of it. The cops couldn't finger the guy. This particular story had just gotten better. Now *my* hair was standing on end.

A couple of the soot-covered torch blazers dropped what they were doing. Pushed all the slack-jawed gawkers behind the barricades. I figured if I was going to get my chance to get closer, this was it.

Soon as the hose jockeys went past me, I vaulted the

barricades myself and went in for a closer gander.

Too late! One of the boys in raincoats spotted me. "Hey, Chief! That guy just jumped the barricade! Stop him!"

I tried to make some ground, but the Chief was faster than I figured. He barreled his husky form right in my path. Then jabbed a cigar-thick index finger right into my chest like he was drilling for oil.

"Hey you!" he demanded. "Where you think you're going?"

I flashed my credentials and got straight to the point. "Tom Miller from the *LA Chronicle*. Is this the work of the arsonist who's been terrorizing the city?"

The Chief didn't take too kindly to my line of questioning. I couldn't blame him. He had bigger fish to fry. "Go chase an ambulance!" he barked. "Can't you see I'm trying to keep this blaze from spreading?"

Just then, two small voices called out from over our heads. None of us wanted to believe it was what it sounded like. But we all looked up and hoped we were wrong.

"Help! Help!"

There was a pair of young tykes still trapped in the building. They stuck their tiny noggins out of a top floor window. Tried to escape the flames and get some air that didn't burn their poor little throats.

The Chief shouted, "My God, we've got to get those kids out of there! Quick, get a ladder up to that window!"

Two of the water boys ran for the ladder truck. But there was no way they could be fast enough for my taste. Not when the lives of two kiddos were involved.

That's when I threw caution to the wind and hightailed it to the building myself.

If I'd thought about it a second longer, I still probably would have done the same thing. The whole place was ablaze and the chances were I wouldn't make it out alive, either.

But there's times when logic just doesn't enter the equation. And this was one of those times.

I heard the Chief shout after me, "What's that crazy reporter doing? Now we've got *three* people to rescue!"

Soon as I hoofed it through the front portal, the heat just about knocked me out. It was hotter than hellfire inside.

The smoke was so thick you could practically walk on it.

Best I could tell, the place had wooden floors, wooden chair rails, and wooden ceilings. Hardly anything that wouldn't burn.

I pulled my jacket up over my breather and made a break for the stairs. Just as I started up, I said a quick prayer that they wouldn't fall out from under me.

I took the manual escalator two at a time and made it up to the second floor in seconds. Pieces of the ceiling fell all around me like burning hailstones.

But I wasn't about to stop and think about how big of a loon I was. Had to keep going.

I two-stepped it up the last two flights until I finally hit the top floor. The smoke was even thicker and the heat was wearing me down. I knew I only had a few more minutes before we were all barbecue.

I barreled down the hall and lamped the apartment doorway. It was all ablaze, so there was no way I was getting in. Who knew if the kids were even still alive at this point?

I tried the adjoining room and hoped there was a connecting door. No such luck. But the wall was on fire and just might give way.

I grabbed a stuffed chair that was just starting to burn. I hoisted the thing up with everything I had. Hoped the kids were still by the window and didn't want to think about the alternative.

I chucked that big rump cushion as hard as I could.

It smashed part of the way through. Got stuck between the plaster and the lathing strips.

The chair made a big enough dent that I was able to kick it the rest of the way and make a good-sized hole. I peered through the smoke and glimmed the kids.

They were on the floor by the window. Not moving. Not good.

Hoped I wasn't too late. I shoved my six-foot-frame through the burning hole and crashed through. My jacket caught fire, so I yanked it off quick before I turned into a blazing marshmallow myself.

I rushed over to the kids and hoped for the best. Still

breathing. Thank God! I scooped the little moppets up, one in each arm, and carefully went back the way I came.

Think I only hit three steps total on the way back down. I barely remember any of it. Saw even less. My only thought was to get those two out before the whole thing came crashing down.

CHAPTER TWO

THE CHIEF was still trying to get a ladder up to the window when we barreled out the doorway. He looked like Santa Claus had just dropped on his front porch. "I — I don't believe it! It's that crazy reporter! He's got the kids!"

The fire snuffers and the screaming mother rushed over and grabbed the tykes. She'd run down to the market for just a few minutes.

Only I wasn't in any condition to complain. I needed air. Fresh, cool air that didn't burn when it went down. I took a dive right there on the pavement.

Just then, the whole igloo melted in a giant heap behind me.

I PROBABLY should have gone to the bandage factory. My arm and my back were a little scorched, but nothing that a little iodine wouldn't fix later. But aside from rescuing those kids, I hadn't run into that blaze for nothing.

I had a story to write. One I hoped my new editor would notice.

I hightailed it over to the nearest squawk box. Despite all the smoke I'd already inhaled, I stuck a gasper in my yap and set fire to it. I needed it bad.

I fumbled in my pockets for some change. Then dialed up the copy editor. Dictated the whole thing for the evening edition. He thought I was making up the heroics. But I assured him I had the burns to prove it.

Figured I'd earned a stiff drink before heading back to the office, so I stopped off at a nearby gin mill and threw back a swig.

The bartender knew that wouldn't be enough, so he passed me another. After a few more, I was ready to hit the skids. I hoped my story had gotten some attention.

Little did I know.

The whole floor jumped up and applauded as soon as I ankled my soot-covered form through the portal. I'd never gotten so many hand-shakes and "atta-boys" in my life.

Everybody jumped up from their typewriters and crowded around me. You'd have thought Lindbergh had just landed.

But then the boss trotted in and he didn't look too jake. Threw a quick damper on the whole shebang.

Looked like it might be time to sharpen my pencil elsewhere.

"Miller!" he shouted.

Hal Jenkins was a newsman to the bone. Short, round in the middle, shaped like a bowling pin. The few hairs still on the top of his head looked like they'd been drawn on. Could barely see through his half-glasses because of the fingerprints.

Jenkins was as old and crusty as a broken down covered wagon. He'd started in the newspaper business when he was just a kid back in Chicago, selling headlines on the street corner and clawing his way up from there.

All I could do was snap to attention. "Yes sir, Mr. Jenkins?"

He paced around like he was sizing me up for a noose. "I realize you're new, but when I hired you, I thought you understood that we just *report* the news around here. We don't *make* it!"

Some editors didn't like hotshot reporters. Looked like Jenkins was one of 'em. I'd definitely overplayed my hand. All I could do was state my case and hope for the best.

"Well, I apologize for that, Sir. But when I saw those kids, I just — "

Jenkins let out a big belly laugh that nearly made me drop my choppers. "Congratulations, Miller! That was first rate! Fine job, a real fine job!"

Looked like I had impressed the boss after all. He glowed like a schoolgirl on her first date.

"This is our best front page story yet! 'CHRONICLE REPORTER SAVES KIDS IN BURNING BLAZE!' Not only that, but you made the front page of every other paper in this city, too!"

Jenkins grabbed a copy of the late edition and thrust it into my mitts. Sure enough, not only did I have the byline on the top story, but I *was* the top story. Couldn't have asked for more than that.

Jenkins turned to hustle out then got stopped by a quick idea. "Say, Miller... how'd you like to come to a party to-night?"

Fiesta with the boss and his cronies didn't sound like a bad idea. This day was just getting better. "Sure," I chirped back. "But if you don't mind, I'd like to go home and change first."

Jenkins let out a chuckle like I was the turkey who'd just showed up for Thanksgiving dinner. "Certainly! You don't want to meet W.H. looking like *that*!"

He let out another good belly laugh and slapped me on the back (which didn't feel too good). Left me puzzled as he chuckled his way back to his office. It had all sounded aces, so I wanted to know why I suddenly had egg on my puss.

So I grabbed one of my compadres, Gil Merton. He was a heavyset fellow with thick glasses and thinning hair.

"Say, who's W.H.?" I queried.

CHAPTER THREE

"WHO'S W.H.?" Gil had the same goofy look, but luckily didn't waste any time spelling it out.

"W.H. Harper! You *work* for him! He owns the *Chronicle*! Pal, you are definitely on your way up!"

Oh, *that* W.H.

Of course, I knew the moniker. Who didn't? I just wasn't used to hearing it without the surname attached.

W.H. Harper was the biggest newspaper fat cat in the country. He owned papers in New York, Chicago, San Francisco, Los Angeles, and all points in between. Not to mention magazines, radio stations, and picture production.

I turned around to find Jenkins' little secretary, Miss Janet Gronchi, staring me down.

She was a mousy little cupcake with a sweet little chassis and a cold expression. Could've given Buster Keaton a run for his money. The name sounded Italian, but she wasn't anything like the dago wrens I knew back East.

If she'd ever let her dark hair down out of that tight bun and lost the horn-rimmed cheaters, she might have been a real cutie. But Hell would have to ice over first.

She handed me an index card. I might've been the hero of the day, but you'd never tell it from her expression. Or lack thereof.

"What's this?" I queried.

"The address to Mr. Harper's residence," she answered. "It's on Palisades Beach Road in Santa Monica. Do you need directions?"

"No, sweetheart, I think I can find it," I chirped. Gave her a little wink as I took the card. But there was no melting that bonnet.

She asked, "Do you have a suit any nicer than the ones you've worn to work? I assume you don't own a tuxedo. It's a black tie affair. But considering the circumstances of your invitation, a well-pressed, dark suit will suffice."

She had a way of asking a question and insulting you at the same time. Lovely quality for a dame.

I thanked her for the fashion tips and pulled a pair of gaspers from my pocket. Before I could get them burning, she turned on her heel and sashayed back to her desk.

She may have been straight as an arrow, but that walk sure had some swing. Had to be for my benefit, I was sure.

I ankled out the portal and took the jalopy back to my apartment stash. I still had an appointment with a cold shower and a bottle of iodine.

Those days I was holed up in the Bellem Building down on Hill Street. Two rooms, fifth floor. No Taj Mahal, but it was close to work, cheap on rent, and had hot water. Most of the time, anyways.

Across the street was a small-time movie house. I could see the marquis outside my window. For some reason, it only played pictures that had aged a little. Even Silents from time to time. Wasn't sure why, but I had my suspicions.

Figured one night I'd catch a flick there when I didn't have anything better to do. But days like that were hard to come by.

And I wanted to keep it that way.

After a cool shower, it was time for the iodine. That hurt even worse than the burns, but a glass of giggle juice and another gasper helped take the edge off.

The minx was right about me not owning a tux. But I had a dark suit that I reserved for weddings and funerals. I got out the hot iron and made sure my creases were sharp as a blade. Then I finished getting dolled up, grabbed my lid, and hopped in my bucket for the drive out to the ocean.

I knew the way. The Santa Monica Pier had been my first stop after hitting the West Coast. Thanks to Uncle Sam, I'd seen the Atlantic from both sides. I'd been itching to touch the Pacific for a change, just to say I'd done it.

Soon as I'd gotten got off the bus, I didn't even stop to get my own set of wheels. I'd hopped straight on the Red Car and rode it all the way to the end.

Spent the whole afternoon just taking in the sights (not to mention all the beautiful quails in two-piece swimmers), smelling the salt air, and even a few rides on the Blue Streak Racer.

It had felt like I was back at Coney Island. Felt real good and then some.

After three years of freezing my keister off fighting the Nazis, it'd been just what I needed. Just like summer on Brighton Beach. And out here it lasted all year long. My idea of paradise.

I just didn't know it would be so deceptive.

CHAPTER FOUR

FORTY-FIVE minutes later, I pulled my bucket into the driveway of the "Beach House." If I'd had any illusions of actually fitting it, they were gone that second. Mine was the only jalopy that didn't have a chauffeur.

It was a white, three-story mansion that looked like it had been picked up from the Old South and dropped right there on the beach. Built on nearly five acres, the place had 34 bedrooms. Not to mention three guest houses, two swimming pools, tennis courts, and a dog kennel bigger than my whole wigwam.

I made note of everything as I went inside. Who knew when I'd see digs like these again? The bootlick at the front door tried to give me some grief. But when I gave him my name, he ushered me right on through with smiles and apologies.

Gronchi was waiting for me in the foyer. Even dolled up she didn't look much different. Her dress was black and sleek, but still covered her diminutive form from head to toe. And with a long, black shawl to cover it even more.

I figured if she was out of her native habitat, I might have a shot at loosening her up a little. But she wasn't slipping her cage anytime soon.

"About time you got here," she piped. "Follow me. Jenkins is waiting."

"Yes, Ma'am," I saluted. She just rolled her glims and led

me into the palace.

The bulk of the party was congregated in the main room. It had the same plantation feel as the outside. Like Harper had just bought the entire state of Georgia.

The giant glass doors opened to a view of the pools and the beach where the rest of the crowd communed outside. The sounds of the ocean complimented the beat from the orchestra playing at the far end of the room.

The room was packed with black ties and fancy dress gowns. I'd never seen so many gorgeous janes in my life. But the room had all kinds.

There were a few gals that wanted to be boys and a few boys who were just as dandy and perfumed as the girls. The only common denominator was that, with the exception of a precious few, everyone was really young or doing their darnedest to look it.

Finally, I spotted Jenkins and he rushed over to great me. Dressed in his penguin outfit, he looked even more like a bowling pin. He grabbed my mitt and shook it good, grinning like he'd just won the lottery.

Jenkins said, "Miller, so glad you're here! I want you to meet Mr. Harper. Come right this way."

Gronchi offered me one bit of advice. "Don't blow it."

Still in his firm grip, Jenkins drug me across the room to a throng of sycophants. I didn't have any trouble picking out Harper.

Of course, I'd seen his picture before. But even without that, there was no mistake. He was the guy in the middle surrounded by all the bootlickers and beautiful quails.

Harper was a big old geezer with a face like a horse and a belly the size of a steamer. From the looks of the young blonde cutie on his arm, and the house, and the paper, I figured he must have a pretty big wallet.

He'd left Mrs. Harper and the (by then grown) kids back in New York while he added West Coast holdings to his already huge empire. But mostly he just played footsie in the sun. He'd constructed the "beach house" for his cutie to go with the other spread he'd built for her in Beverly Hills.

Jenkins nervously interrupted, "Mr. Harper, I want to introduce you to Tom Miller, our new star reporter."

Harper looked up with a big grin, then shook my duke even harder than Jenkins had. His cutie even gave me a smile.

Harper said: "Miller, I can't thank you enough for saving those children. And for giving us one of the best front page stories we've had in years!"

He gave me a big pat on the back. I only winced a little.

"Would you mind sharing your exploits with us again?" he asked. "I think it would be much more exciting to hear it directly in person."

"Yeah," I answered. "Sure thing."

So that was it. I was the night's entertainment. Brought out to perform for Harper and his little blonde trick. Like a trained circus monkey that rides a bike and balances a banana on its head.

No matter. This guy was the big boss and he held my whole career between his two fingers like a pea. If this was what it took to get a boost, I was gonna give them their money's worth.

I went ahead and took my jacket off. I recounted the whole story. Detail for detail. Beat for beat. Only goosed the facts a little, since my first version was already in print.

Then it was time for the big finish. I jerked off my Oxford. Popped a few buttons. Down to my undershirt to show the burns on my arm and my shoulders. Even flexed the guns for good measure. The older women shrieked in embarrassment. The younger ones let out a different sound.

Harper straightened up and applauded. His cutie did, too. Just the reaction I was looking for.

"Jenkins, this is some reporter you've got here!" he shouted. Then he grabbed my paw and shook it again. "You keep up the good work, Miller. Keep up the good work!"

And that was it. Show over. Time to move on. No time to even take my bows.

Jenkins tugged me aside. Glad, but more nervous than he was before. "Well, Miller, that was some performance."

"Think Harper liked it?" I asked.

"Yes, I course. He seemed quite thrilled. But what'dya say you keep your shirt on next time, okay?"

"Sure thing, Boss," I promised.

THE CITY BURNS AT NIGHT

Jenkins patted me on the arm, then steered me in the direction of the punch bowl. "Go enjoy yourself, Miller. Have a good time. You've earned it." He gave me another pat, then disappeared back into the group of bootlickers surrounding Harper.

I looked around for Gronchi, but didn't spot her anywhere. Still, I was sure her disapproving glare couldn't be far off.

I tried to pitch woo to some of the janes who'd watched the show, but they just smiled and went back to their rich suitors. Despite the audience reaction, I was still the trained monkey. And you don't mess around with the help.

So, I made for the snack table to grab some peanuts. The spread was to die for. But it was nothing compared to the demure little cupcake that stood near the punch bowl.

She had a figure more delicious than anything on the table. Big, bright eyes and the sweetest smile I'd ever seen. Rosy lips, soft brown hair neatly combed back. The picture of innocence. She'd have looked more out of place than I did if she hadn't been so beautiful.

Things were looking up.

CHAPTER FIVE

I WAS about to make my introduction when she beat me to it. "You must be the hero everyone is talking about."

"Yeah." I asked, "How'd you know?"

"Well," she answered with a smile that would make a rabbi bluish. "Everyone here is either in the movies or a business tycoon, and you don't look like either one."

I didn't know if that was a compliment or an insult. "Meaning I'm the only one not decked out to the nines."

Her face turned redder than her lipstick. "I'm sorry, I didn't mean to embarrass you."

My turn to feel like a heel. This wren really was sweet. The genuine article. "It's all right, don't worry about it."

I gently offered a mitt and introduced myself. "Tom Miller. *L.A. Chronicle.*"

She gave me her gentle little wing. I'd never felt hands that soft before. "Trudy Wilkes."

Nice name. I did the gentlemanly thing and gave her dainty duke a little kiss.

She gave me a little smile back. "That was a very brave thing you did. Most people would have been too frightened."

"Well, danger has always intrigued me," I confessed. "Sometimes I go looking for it, just for the excitement."

"Is that why you became a reporter?" she asked.

I'd never thought of it that way, but, yeah. I told her she was probably right. Insightful, too. "Would you care for some punch, Miss Wilkes?" I asked her.

"You can call me Trudy," she offered. "But no thank you. I'm sure it's spiked, and I don't drink." Strike one.

I fished a couple of gaspers out of my coat pocket. I was about to light one up when she put the kibosh on that, too.

"No thank you. I don't smoke, either." Strike two.

I was running out of options and thinking maybe I should head for greener pastures when I took my last swing at bat. "Would you care to dance, then?"

"Yes, I would." She smiled. Base hit.

I took that soft little wing again and led her out to the dance floor. We were surrounded by other couples. Many of whom I recognized from my performance.

It was a soft, bouncy tune. Perfect for a "getting-to-know-you" trot. Not too romantic, but not too jittery, either.

I tried to think of just the right thing to say. No worries, though. She was quick with the conversation. "Are you new in town?"

"Yeah," I spilled. "Just moved out here a month ago. From back East."

"Well then, if you're going to be a reporter in Hollywood, you need to find out who is who."

"Think you could help a fellow out?" I grinned.

She gave me a sweet smile again. "See that man?"

She pointed out a tall, broad-shouldered fellow with wavy, grey hair and a studious expression. Looked like a real bigshot. "That's William Wade, the film director."

Then she turned my gaze towards a fellow in big glasses, a long cigar, and skin too tanned even for Malibu. Another bigshot. But nothing like we have back home. "Over there is George Mitchell. He's a producer."

Next she steered me to a wiry, Jewish fellow with a pinched face. "And that man is Thomas Feinstein. He's in banking. He mostly finances films."

Trudy was about to point me towards some other high-muck-a-muck when I caught sight of *something else* that really got my attention.

"Who is *that*?"

Trudy had to pick my jaw up off the floor. "Don't you recognize her?"

My glims had locked on a jane that had just sauntered in. The most scorching blonde I'd ever seen. She had a body that would tempt Adam back into Eden for more apples. She was just like a high-speed drive down Mulholland. Dangerous and full of curves.

Her long bangs covered one eye and the rest of her face looked like a goddess. She wore a slinky black dress that hugged her like a Latin lover. Had a figure that would make Venus jealous. And stems that would make roses sit up and beg.

"She an actress?" I gurgled. I had to go to the galloping tintypes more often.

"Of course," she chided. "She won an Oscar for *The Sins of Aphrodite*. Don't you go to the movies?"

Trudy said it like it was a crime. Judging by the evidence, I'd say I was due for twenty years with no chance of parole.

"No," I admitted. "I think maybe the last picture I saw was *silent*."

Had no idea what I'd been missing. And how. Clearly I was hungry to know more, so Trudy went ahead and filled me in.

"Her name is Irene Faye. She married a producer, Derek Saltzman." She glanced around the room. "I'd point him out, but I don't see him around anywhere. She was really big for a while."

"So, what happened?" I asked. Perplexed as to how a quail like that could ever hit the skids. "Why isn't she big anymore?"

"She broke the rules," Trudy continued. "She caught Saltzman with another woman. And then went crying to the press. She tried to ruin his career, but it backfired on her. She was a nobody when she married him, and without his support, the studio won't touch her."

"So, they're still hitched?" I asked, trying not to let the disappointment show through.

"Yes, but not really," Trudy explained. "He's got the house in Malibu, and she's got the one in Beverly Hills. I'd stay clear of her, though. Saltzman is extremely jealous."

So I'd been warned. All I could do was shake my noggin. "Some town. Sure is a shame, though."

"What's that?" she asked.

"There's a beautiful beach out there and we're cooped up inside. What do you say we ankle our way out of this monkey cage and go for a stroll?" I suggested.

She gave me a suspicious look, like a mouse wary of a trap. "I don't know."

"Come on, Doll," I told her and stuck my paws in my pockets. "You can trust me. Honest Injun. Mitts to myself."

Of course, I couldn't say anything for the other guests. Soon as we exited the back portal and made for the sand, we chanced more than one couple *en flagrante* out on the back lawn. She turned to rush back to the barn, but I grabbed her by the wing.

"Hey, don't mind these bozos," I told her and tugged her the rest of the way down the wooden path to the shoreline. I let go as soon as we reached the beach. Kept a respectable distance with my dukes back in their holsters.

"See, honest Injun. Just like I said."

She flashed me an innocent smile. Even in the moonlight, I could see she was warming up. Sometimes, it just takes a gentleman. I should try it more often.

Have to admit, with the moon reflecting on the ocean and the waves crashing into the shore, it was pretty darn romantic. I was certainly getting ideas, but it was better to keep them to myself.

We weren't the only couple down there, but we were the only ones who weren't a couple. She was still a little uneasy. Kept talking about the movie biz, who the power players were. She pointed out the identities of our fellow beachcombers and the couples we'd seen getting serious on the lawn. This sweet little jane was like a walking *Who's Who*.

But I was interested in turning the conversation in another direction. "There is one person here you haven't told me about."

"Who?" she asked.

"You."

She turned her shade of lipstick again.

"Me? I'm an actress. Well, I'm trying to become an actress." I could tell there was more to her story. She looked about nervously and finally fessed up.

"Actually, I sort of crashed this party. My friend, Anita, is working here to-night as a hostess and she snuck me in. I was hoping to meet someone important. You know, who could help me with my career."

"Trying to get discovered. I see." Everybody has an angle. Especially out here. "Why not just hang out at Schwab's?"

"You mean like Lana Turner?" she asked with a dainty laugh.

"What's so funny?" I queried.

"I work there, actually," she explained. "At the lunch counter. Dishing sandwiches, coffee, and ice cream sundaes until something better comes along. I served Ava Gardner one time. She's really sweet."

"Resourceful girl," I commented.

"Oh, and Lana Turner wasn't actually discovered there," she chuckled. "That's just the Hollywood press version. She was really discovered at the Top Hat Café down the street. I guess somebody thought Schwab's made a better story."

"Not the folks who run the Top Hat," I replied.

She let out a sweet laugh in agreement.

"So how do you know so much about Hollywood?" I asked.

"I just read the trades and the gossip pages," she told me.

Looked like I could use some tutoring. "Well, I see I've got a lot to learn about this town. Wonder if you could fill me in some time. Say... Saturday night over dinner?"

"Well," she confessed again, "Normally I don't accept invitations from men I've just met, and especially on such short notice. Maybe some other time?"

"Of course, Doll. I understand," I fibbed.

Part of me wanted to ditch this gal, but if I'd let her go, who knew what vulture would sink his claws into her. She was too sweet by far. A rare jewel that you just don't toss aside.

We walked down the beach for a good while longer. She filled me in on how she'd fallen in love with the galloping tintypes growing up in Dayton, had studied to be a secretary, and placed second in a beauty contest. I couldn't imagine the gal who'd come in first.

We'd just about made it back to the house (fortunately,

the back yard was now clear of over-amorous couples) when we were greeted by a cute, blonde hostess with an anxious smile and ideas in her head. I'd glimmed her serving drinks earlier. This had to be "Anita."

"Hey, I've been looking all over for you," she said, giving me the up and down before turning back to Trudy. "Look, you think you can find another ride home? I can give you the money for a taxi if you need it."

Her anxious smile got bigger as she nodded towards the slicked-down, Producer-type who hovered behind her.

TRUDY was at a loss for words. Like a gal who'd been ditched at the side of the road without a suitcase or a bus ticket home.

"Don't worry, I'll get her home," I piped in.

I didn't know who was more thankful, Anita or Trudy. Or me, for that matter.

I led Trudy out to the front drive and waited for the valet to bring my jalopy around. I think she was surprised by its *ordinariness*. But was polite enough not to say anything. Another sign she was a true angel.

I opened the passenger door to let her in. I wouldn't have been surprised if she'd insisted on the back. But she thanked me kindly and got in anyways. "Where to, Sweetheart?" I asked.

"West Hollywood, on Wilshire. It's a boarding house for young women," she directed.

Her anxiety seemed to come back, and I couldn't blame her. I don't think she'd ever gotten the ditch before, and she didn't know me from Adam. But I was determined to stay the gentleman.

"Don't worry, Baby," I reassured her. "I'll have you back home in no time." I put my bucket in gear and pointed it back towards the city.

"I don't think Mrs. Young will like me coming back without Anita, she fretted. "She's going to be awfully sore."

"That's Anita's problem," I told her.

Trudy filled me in on "the rules" for staying there, and how Anita was always bucking the system. I didn't say anything. But thought I wouldn't be surprised if one day

Anita turned up as to-morrow's headline.

You never know with gals like that.

Seemed like no time before we pulled up at her place. It was one of those big, sprawling Victorian-style homes you don't see too many of out here any more.

The Youngs had money at one time, but had to open it up to boarders after the Crash of '29. That's when Mr. Young decided to go downtown and take a short walk off a tall building.

I opened her car door and escorted Trudy up to the front portico. It was a warm Spring night. The crickets were chirping and the moon was full.

Not as romantic as the beach, but enough to incite the birds and the bees. They were buzzing all around in the moonlight. We stopped on the porch and she turned to look back at me with those big, beautiful peepers.

"Tom, I can't thank you enough for everything you've done for me to-night. You really are a true gentleman. Mother was sure I'd never meet anyone like that here, but you've certainly proven her wrong."

The sincerity in her voice went straight to the heart. Made me glad I'd kept her unspoiled.

"You know how I said I don't accept invitations from men I've just met?" she reminded me. "Well, something tells me I should make an exception this time."

She flashed a smile that melted me down to my brogans. I was ready to seal the date with a kiss. But I was smart enough to know not to ruin it.

"See you this Friday?" she asked.

I looked back at her with surprise. She'd upped me by a day. Subtle, Baby. Very subtle.

"You got it, Doll," I told her.

You don't just throw away a precious gem.

CHAPTER SIX

NEXT morning, I hit the newsroom early. After my command performance at the party, I didn't want Jenkins to think I'd gotten a swelled head. I was still a stand-up guy. Good thing I did, too, because I had a visitor waiting for me as soon as I ankled my way in.

He flashed his tin and introduced himself. Detective Hap Underwood, Los Angeles PD. He was unlike any tin shamus I'd ever met — immaculate, light-blue suit and white Panama lid. Fairly young guy, about my age.

Had a laid-back style that would put most anyone at ease. But made me think there was a lot more going on under that brim than meets the eye.

He fingered a copy of the morning edition. "You Tom Miller?"

We danced through the pleasantries then got down to brass tacks. I knew he wasn't there for a rehash of what he'd already read in the headlines.

"I'd like to ask you a few questions," he said, glancing around, hoping for someplace more private.

I called over to Gronchi. "Hey, Sweetheart, Jenkins around this morning?"

"He's down in the press room," she said.

"I need to borrow his office for a few minutes," I told her.

She gave me a knowing nod and I led Underwood into

Jenkins' quarters. He leaned against the desk as I shut the door.

Jenkin's office looked like any other city editor's office I'd been in. Small, cramped, and cluttered to the walls with yesterday's news and to-morrow's headlines.

"So, what made you hightail it into that fire?" he queried.

"There were kids inside," I told him. "The hose jockeys were taking too long. Somebody had to do it."

"Right." He gave me a suspicious look. Same look I give out every day when *I* ask the questions.

"How long you say you've been in LA?" he asked.

So, he'd already tabbed me as an out-of-towner. Sharp guy. But back then I was pretty easy to spot. Practically smelled of bus fumes.

"Couple of weeks," I told him. I knew what he was getting at. "These blazes started before I even got off the Greyhound, in case you're wondering. I can show you my bus ticket."

"Don't worry, you're not a suspect," he grinned. I knew better than to believe him.

"But tell me, you see anything at the fire, inside the building, anywhere, that might be a clue as to who did it? I promise, I won't spill it to the other papers."

Wish I'd had such a clue. "Afraid I was too busy worrying about those kids," I told him. "And staying alive myself."

"I can understand that," he said, clearly not believing me.

Still, I dug through my noodle to see if anything came loose. I make it a rule to stay on the right side of the law whenever possible. In my game, that can come in handy.

That's when a thought occurred to me. "You know, now that I think about it, I did notice one thing. When I first went in, it smelled like kerosene."

His lamps lit up on that one. Just for a hot second.

"Well, Miller," he said, sticking out his fin. "Thank you for your time. Pleasure meeting you."

I went ahead and shook his mitt, but I still couldn't help feeling he was sizing me up for a pair of nippers. "That was a pretty brave thing to do. Anyone who risks his neck for kids is a-okay in my book."

Okay, that last one was sincere. Thought maybe I was

misreading this guy.

"You come up with anything else, I'd appreciate it if you'd let me know. Maybe I can throw something your way, too."

"Like a suspect?" I asked.

He just grinned, tipped his lid, and let himself out.

I let him get a good ways down the hall before I sailed back to Gronchi's desk. "You get that?"

"Of course, every word," she said, holding up her notepad with four pages of fresh shorthand. I'd only been on the job a day or two before I learned that Gronchi hears every word in Jenkins' office. Best place to have a *private conversation*.

It was only a few more minutes before the boss himself galloped back in. Even though he was long out of his tux, he still looked like he'd been there all night. Might have been for all I knew.

He conferred with Gronchi for a moment, then launched into his cave. Gave me a quick nod as he disappeared through the portal. I followed him in.

"So, I hear you met Detective Underwood this morning?" he asked.

"Yeah," I told him. "Asked me about the blaze yesterday. I'll let Gronchi fill you in on all the details."

"He's a good-enough fellow," Jenkins clued me. "Straight on the up-and-up. You do right by him, he'll do the same for you."

That was how I'd sized him up, too.

Then Jenkins got to the point. "Listen, Miller, thanks to your bravado at the fire, I'm putting you on the Arson story."

I thanked him politely, but all the little people that live inside me were jumping up and down. This was it.

I was stepping up.

He turned to a map of the city that was pinned up on his wall. Red tacks marked all the joints that had gone up in flames.

"This shows all the places that the Arsonist has hit, but there just doesn't seem to be any sense to it."

His stubby finger guided me along to each one. "There's an office building, an abandoned warehouse, a producer's house, and then the apartment building the other night. I just can't figure it."

All I could do was state the obvious. "Just looks like we've got some lunatic running around with a pack of matches."

Jenkins agreed. But he wanted more than the obvious from me. He wanted answers. Or at least a way to get them.

I started with square one. "Why don't I hang out at the clubhouse this afternoon and see what I can dig up. The cops always know more than they're telling. I'm sure somebody down there will sing for a price."

Jenkins gave in to a broad smile. "Miller, I like your style. Just keep me informed."

Soon as I was back at my desk, Gronchi was glaring down at me like Sister Eugenia with a ruler. And proved I was right about her keeping an eye on me.

"So, how'd it go with that young lady you met last night?"

Trudy. What was there to say? We'd bumped gums for a good while. But it was all a trip for biscuits. "It was all jake. She's pretty nice, and a real doll, too. But..."

"But what?"

"She's kind of a goody-two-shoes," I spilled. "Doesn't drink, doesn't smoke, doesn't go out to clubs. She wouldn't even let me kiss her goodnight. I like a girl with more of an... adventurous streak."

"Oh, there's plenty of adventurous gals around here, you just found the only one that isn't."

Not including herself, apparently.

Then she just shook her little noggin. "I'd say she did a good job of getting your attention, though."

"Oh, yeah?" I queried.

That's when Gronchi laid it all out for me. "I'm sure you put it together pretty fast that she was a *nice* girl. And if you didn't, then Jenkins hired the wrong reporter."

Yeah, she had a point there.

"Anyway," she continued, "there were a ton of *eligible* young women at that party. Any other lug would have ditched her for greener pastures. But you saw her *home*."

Okay, so Gronchi was right. Trudy did make an impression on me.

And a big one at that.

THE CITY BURNS AT NIGHT

BUT I didn't have time to worry about that. I had a story to write. And at this point I was just staring at a blank page. So, I high-tailed it over to Spring Street in my jalopy to see what I could dig up.

Back then the LAPD was housed in the north wing of the Los Angeles City Hall. Looks like a giant mausoleum. Just needs a big graveyard to go with it. Hoped this wouldn't be an omen.

There was a gaggle of my fellow news hounds outside trading war stories and chewing the fat. Since I'd just made the front page of their respective papers, I can't say they were exactly thrilled to see me.

But I knew if I was going to work in this town, I needed to make nice with the competition. You never know when you might need to jump ship. Or someone to vouch for you.

But there was one who actually gave me a smile and meant it. A hotshot reporter for the *Tribune*. And one hell of a looker to boot.

CHAPTER SEVEN

SHE WAS a raven-haired wren by the name of Flora Mason. I'd heard about her just as soon as I hit town. One hot ticket in high heels.

After she flashed her pearly whites, she nodded me aside for some extra gab.

"Hey Firebug, what's cooking?" she asked. "You always play the hero? Or was this just a one-time engagement?"

"When I see kids trapped in a burning building," I told her, "I don't care who makes the headlines."

Which was at least partially true. I may not care, I just prefer it to be me.

"Man with a big heart," she nodded. "I like that."

It was obvious she was sizing me up. It was even more obvious I was doing the same.

"Judging by your grand performance and that encore at Harper's party last night," she informed me, "I'd say Jenkins put you on the arson story."

She had me over a barrel on that one. But I wasn't about to admit it. I sure would have remembered seeing her at the Plantation. But the quail obviously had me pegged.

"You ever want an encore of your own," I told her, "just give me a whistle."

She just shook her pretty noggin and laughed. "Oh, I wasn't there, Pinkerton. But I heard all about it. I have my sources."

Right. She definitely had me over a barrel. And this time she knew it, too.

That's when she dropped the pretense and got to the point. "I just want you to know, this is my story. Anyone in this town breaks into the big time, it's going to be me. Got it?"

"Worried I'll step on your painted toenails?"

"Not hardly," she huffed.

Then she leaned in close with that dazzling smile. And the full force of her femininity. "I'm just giving you fair warning. Stay out of my way."

Then she backed away and sashayed off. And threw a little extra swing in her chassis. "You do that and we'll get along just fine."

I TROTTED inside and made my way to the detective squad. All the shamuses, Underwood included, were out to lunch. Found a young bull, Rigby, still fresh out of the Academy and wet behind the lobes. He was as thin and gangly as he was eager to please.

Told him I'd make it worth his while to help a fellow out. Now and in the future. He showed me into the file room.

"The records are in here," Officer Rigby whispered quietly as he showed me in. "Now I can only give you ten minutes. If we get caught, I'll lose my job. Or worse."

Worse was right, but the less he knew, the better. I thanked him and slipped him a bill. "Thanks, Officer. I hope this will make up for your trouble."

That brought a quick smile to his kisser. "Hey, a sawbuck. Thanks, pal!"

He shut the door and let me get to work. I went straight for the As. Arson. Bingo! What do you know? Right in front. Good thing I wasn't looking for a Zookeeper.

I pulled out the folder and glimmed the pages. There was a bit of cartography just like the one on Jenkins' wall. Plus newspaper clippings about each of the jobs. Including the one by yours truly. And I was willing to bet even money that Flora Mason's fingerprints were all over them.

But did they have a suspect?

I dug through some more and found a rap sheet in the

back of the file. That's when I hit pay dirt.

Frank Kellman. Convicted of arson, served four years. Got out six months ago. This was looking very promising.

Had his mug shot, too. Beefy guy, dark hair, steely eyes. Scar that ran down his right cheek. Not the kind of guy you want to pal around with. Last known address was an apartment stash on South La Brea.

I skimmed through the rest and finally hit on something that clicked near the end. Last employer was a guy named "Derek Saltzman."

Knew I'd heard that name recently, but couldn't place it. Got out my notepad and jotted down everything I could. The clock was ticking.

Stuck the file back in the drawer just in time for young Rigby to chase me off. I tipped him another sawbuck on my way out of the portal. Figured I'd probably need his services again and wanted to make sure he'd be agreeable.

As I ankled it out of City Hall, I racked my brain muscles trying to remember where I'd heard that name before. In the meantime, I figured I'd take a peek around Kellman's old digs.

I HOPPED back in my jalopy and rode Wilshire all the way out toward the Tar Pits. Half hour or so later I pulled up in front of a two-story, tan stucco building. Spanish-style roof. Kind you see a lot of in Los Angeles.

The landlady, Mrs. Kratz, was a nice enough old broad. I'd had many an old lady shut a door in my face. But this old gal just wanted someone to listen.

She'd moved out West from Chicago ten years earlier and had two daughters. A couple of real cuties from the pictures she showed me. Both were trying to break into the picture business. "Aren't they just lovely?" she asked.

Had to agree. Hoped either one would stop by while I was there.

She'd rented out Kellman's old stash years ago, but still had some of his things stuck in a closet. Nobody ever came back to claim them. Not until the cops had been there a week before me.

"I keep everything old tenants leave behind," she

confessed as she showed me to her storage closet. "Keep it all stored here, organized and labeled. You never know when someone will come back to claim something. It's happened before, you know."

I tried to wave her off. But that old bird must've been desperate for conversation because she never stopped bending my ear.

"Had one tenant come back six years later, just for a pair of shoes. Must have been something about those shoes to come back after six years. I'm surprised they still fit."

Kellman had left behind a suit, neatly pressed. She hung it in a bag to keep the moths out.

"Nice suit of clothes there," she pointed out.

Odd that he'd be back in town and not come back for that. The rest I could understand. But not the duds. I made a note on where he'd bought it.

The rest of his things were all in a box. I kneeled down to rummage through it. In addition to a razor, comb, and that sort of thing, there was a shoebox full of newspaper clippings.

All of them about Irene Faye.

Another shoebox was full of matchbooks from all the digs around town: The Brown Derby, Don the Beachcomber, Musso and Frank's, Perino's, Slapsy Maxie's, the Trocadero. You name it. Figured for a firebug. Surprised the cops didn't take those with them.

Had quite a few from King's Tropical Inn over on Washington Blvd. in Culver City. Guessed that was his favorite. Mrs. Kratz confirmed it. "Oh, Mr. Kellman loved to eat there. A couple times a week, at least. He just loved the dollar twenty-five squab dinner."

Thank goodness this old broad was so nosey. If Kellman were in town, he'd surely drop into his favorite eatery. Maybe I'd catch up with him. If nothing else, I could find out what the hell a "squab" was.

Underneath the shoebox was a lobby card from one of Irene Faye's flickers. And a copy of *Tell-All Magazine* with you-know-who on the front cover. Kellman clearly had a thing for this dame. Who could blame him?

"Mr. Kellman was quite the fan, wasn't he?" Mrs. Kratz

asked in her cheery, sing-song voice. "Used to talk about her all the time."

I gave the rag the once-over. The cover story was about the ravishing Miss Faye stepping out with her chauffeur. With lots of photos of her looking angry, glamorous, or both. All with an emphasis on her ample charms. Then I flipped the page to get the shock of my life.

There was a picture of the beautiful Irene Faye with her supposed Romeo.

Frank Kellman!

CHAPTER EIGHT

I JUST about fell back on my keister. Kellman was the chauffeur?

"That's right," Mrs. Kratz offered. "Mr. Kellman used to work for her husband, Derek Saltzman."

That's when the outline finally fell into place. So Kellman was keeping time with that dangerous blonde twist who'd made my teeth stand on end. It was all starting to make sense!

I asked Mrs. Kratz if I could hang on to the gossip rag. Figured I needed to do more than just look at the pictures. She wasn't too agreeable, but I promised to return it soon.

I pressed her a sawbuck and hitched my bucket over to Pink's for a couple of dogs and some heavy reading. They aren't Nathan's, but they're mighty damn close.

The whole piece played like a soap opera. I could practically hear the organ music grinding in the background. Not to mention the detergent commercials every time I flipped a page.

Seems old Derek liked to step out with the ladies, leaving the poor Mrs. at home all alone. Only she wasn't poor. And she definitely wasn't alone. Dame like that never is.

After I'd gotten my fill of the dogs and the melodrama, I ankled it across the street to the closest squawk box. I stepped inside and yodeled Jenkins.

"Mr. Jenkins, this is Miller. Look, I got a line on the

suspect. His name's Frank Kellman. Used to work for Derek Saltzman as a chauffeur."

"The producer?" Jenkins asked with surprise.

"Yeah," I told him. "I'm heading over there first thing to-morrow."

I could practically hear Jenkins scratching his noodle over the line. "Very interesting, Miller. But you can bet the police have already questioned Saltzman. I doubt you'll be able to get near him."

I wasn't about to let a little thing like that stop me. Running into burning buildings wasn't the only trick up my sleeve.

"Don't worry," I told him. "I didn't get this far in the game by being shy."

WENT back to my apartment stash, torched a gasper and settled down with four fingers in a tumbler. I flipped through the pages of the rag again.

Irene Faye. She was the kind of dame a guy like Kellman would never get a shot at. The way I figured it, he was just lucky (*real* lucky) to be in the right place when she was lonely and looking for evens. It was easy to see why he'd want to come back for seconds.

Even in those newsprint photos on cheap paper, she just leaped off the page and grabbed your attention. I could only imagine the kind of power she had up on the giant screen. That silky, golden hair. Those perfectly soft lips. Those eyes that just stared right through you.

But the part I couldn't get a bead on was the whole arson angle. Was Kellman always a firebug? Did an old habit just get in the way?

Or did Irene Faye kick him to the curb and he reached for a pack of matches?

The dots weren't all connecting. I had some more lines to draw.

EARLY the next morning, I put a call in to Gronchi. Told her not to wait up for me. Instead, I steered my bucket down Melrose, to Saltzman's outfit, Metropolitan Pictures.

It was my first time on a studio lot. I'll admit I wasn't

sure what to expect. I pulled up outside the gate and got stopped by the hired bull. He wasn't the real thing, but I'd soon find out that when you're on the lot, he might as well be.

My press pass and a little palm grease got me in without a hitch. The studio bull directed me to a nearby parking lot. I ditched my bucket and hit the pavement.

Next thing I know I'm walking down a city street. If I didn't know any better, I'd have thought I was back outside the studio. Only the street was too clean. Everything was a little too perfect. And the buildings were only just the front.

There was one other big reminder I wasn't in Kansas anymore: the crumpled remains of the Hollywoodland Sign. It loomed high on the mountainside right behind the studio. You could practically see it from anywhere on the lot.

Wasn't sure how to find Saltzman, but I was sure this wasn't it. He'd either be in an office or on a set somewhere herding the action. Next thing I knew, I was lost in a sea of soundstages. With no idea which way was up.

Finally I just snagged a grizzled Cowboy as he passed me by. I flashed my press pass. "Say, Pal, you know where I can find Derek Saltzman?"

"Afraid I don't rightly know, Partner," he drawled back. Neither did a Saloon Girl, a Roman Soldier, or a pair of Nuns grabbing a smoke.

I saw a young, weasel-faced fellow in a brown tweed suit give me the eye.

Just when I thought I'd been bagged, my luck turned for the better.

I ran into Trudy outside Stage 29. My lamp sockets did a double-take when I saw what she was wearing. Or more accurately, what she wasn't.

It was nothing more than a gold, strapless bikini top with a negligee skirt that was six degrees thinner than tissue paper. Didn't leave much to the imagination. Certainly got me looking forward to our impending date even more.

"Tom! What are you doing here?" she blurted in surprise. She looked a little embarrassed and crossed her arms to cover herself.

"I was about to ask you the same question," I answered. My expression told her I was asking for a whole different reason.

"I'm working," she explained. "As an extra. I'm playing a temple virgin."

Good casting. Though in that outfit, I couldn't see her staying one very long.

"I'm working myself," I told her. "Looking for Derek Saltzman. Any idea where he hangs his lid in this place?"

"Are you on a story?" she asked with a curious smile. The sense of adventure seemed to get to her.

I told her I just needed to ask a few questions then plied her again regarding his whereabouts.

"Oh, I don't know," she confessed. "But I bet Anita does. I've got to get back in. But maybe we can ask her after the next shot."

I remembered the Fair Anita. She was the cute blonde trick who'd ditched Trudy at Harper's party and left her in my care. I owed her one.

Trudy grabbed me by the paw and tugged me through a small gap in a giant warehouse door. I couldn't help but notice again how soft and delicate her dainty little mitt was.

She could have led me anywhere in that moment. Which is pretty much what she did.

She tugged me down a dark, plywood corridor that turned this way and that. Next thing I know, we turn a corner and we're smack in a Roman palace. Complete with a pool and a couple dozen barely dressed beauties.

Felt like I'd died and gone to heaven.

CHAPTER NINE

A MASS of giant lights hung from the ceiling and lit the whole place up just like we were outside. And if it hadn't been for the obviously painted backdrop hanging behind the columns, you'd have believed it, too.

Trudy pressed me towards a back wall and told me to keep quiet. I told her not to worry. Had my press pass in hand just in case.

She gave me a quick smile and rejoined her fellow virgins on the set. Most of whom didn't look nearly as authentic as she did. Especially the lovely young Anita.

Not far from me was the slicked-down, producer-type from the same party.

Two and two told me how they'd gotten the job. I watched Trudy whisper to Anita while the latter made eyes at their benefactor.

Just then, some bald Kraut in a lifeguard chair shouted into a bullhorn. What little noise there was quickly went silent. He was brief and to the point.

"Roll cameras! Action!"

That was when I got my first sight of a real, live movie star. And on her home turf, no less.

It was Myrna Davis. I'd never seen one of her pictures, but I knew who she was. Every red-blooded American male who fought in the war did. Most of us had her picture stuffed in our gear. She'd even come out to the field a few times to entertain the troops. I'd been sorry I'd missed out, but this was more than making up for it.

She was just as beautiful in real life as she was up on the screen. She was dolled up to be an Egyptian Queen. Her sultry, dark hair was cut and braided to match. Sadly, the long, white dress she wore wasn't as revealing as the outfits that surrounded her.

She was quickly followed by a tall, good-looking fellow wearing a Roman tunic. I recognized him, too: Roland Philips was the name. Always thought he looked a bit like a dandy myself. Seeing him up close didn't change my mind.

Philips mooned after her like a lost puppy and confessed his love over and over. She gave him the brush and told him he could have any ten gals there if he'd just powder.

As delectable as Myrna Davis was, I'd have easily taken the deal. But that wasn't the way it read in the script.

After they replayed the scene a dozen times over, the bald Kraut of a Director shouted into his megaphone again. "Cut!"

Looked like a pretty easy job from where I stood. Especially on the eyes.

With the all-clear, Trudy darted back over in my direction. "Mr. Saltzman's office is in the Executive Hall. You just go out past Stage 32. It looks like a big Federal building."

"Thanks, Doll," I said, and gave her the up-and-down one last time. "Still looking forward to our date Friday night."

"I'll be ready," she said. And sounded almost as excited as I was.

I FOUND my way out of the soundstage and hightailed it past Stage 32. With any luck, I'd be chatting with Saltzman momentarily.

Only my luck had completely run out.

Soon as I approached the long, white edifice that looked like it would be right at home in our nation's capital, I found the young, weasel-faced fellow in the brown tweed suit waiting with two big Studio bulls. And a stocky bruiser wearing a suit that cost more than my jalopy. They didn't look happy to see me.

"I understand you're looking for Mr. Saltzman," the

bruiser queried in a heavy Brooklyn accent. I'd find out later his name was Eddie Lennox. He's the one they called when there was a problem. And he didn't need the bulls to back him up.

I flashed my press pass and grinned back, "Sure, Maxie. Just want to ask him a few questions, that's all."

"Regarding?" he shot back.

I tried to play it cute. "A new story I heard he might be working on. Supposed to be a real hot one."

No luck. They weren't buying my ruse for even a second.

The two bulls grabbed me by the collar. Drug me all the way across the lot back to my jalopy. Then they saw to it that I drove right out the gate, too.

Immediately.

I CRUISED down the block to the nearest squawk box. Failure or no, it was time to update Jenkins. The visit hadn't been a total loss.

The fact that Saltzman was avoiding the press told me something. He was involved somehow. And that was reason enough to keep digging. I just needed to turn my shovel in another direction.

I dropped a buffalo and rang Jenkins. "You were right. My studio visit didn't pan out. But don't worry. I've got another idea."

"What's that?" he asked.

"I'm gonna try talking to the Mrs.," I offered.

"I doubt you'll be able to see her, either," Jenkins reasoned.

"Child's play," I told him. "I know an old trick that's sure to get me in. Just need a necklace."

"You plan on buying one?" he asked. I could practically hear the cash registers ringing in his lobes. Palm grease was one expense. Plying with jewelry was a whole other level.

"No," I told him. "There's a cab company just up the street. I'm sure there's one in their Lost and Found I can weasel out of them."

I could hear Jenkins give a quick shout to Miss Gronchi and seconds later came back with Irene Faye's address.

Benedict Canyon Road, Beverly Hills.

Sounded like fun. I'd only driven through the Hills on my way to Santa Monica, so it would be nice to finally stop in for a gander.

I ankled it down the block to the hack stand. The place was filled with yellows, all in various states of repair, but no one around.

I strolled all the way to the back before I glimmed a young quail in the office. She was a nice little jane, if you go for the tomboy type. A little paint on the nails to replace the grease and she might have been a real cutie. She was reading the latest issue of *Tell-All Magazine*.

I rapped on the window to get her attention.

Thought she might jump up out of her seat, but instead she answered without even giving me a slant. "Yeah?" she asked.

I did my best to sell her a bag of goods. "Say, my wife lost a necklace in one of your cabs the other night. Anyways, I was wondering if someone might have found it."

"What's it look like?" she asked, peepers still glued to her yellow rag.

I was hoping she'd just let me eye their stash, but no such luck. Had to give her some details, but not get too specific. "Well, it's about so long... and it has lots of bead things on it."

The dumb act worked. She'd gotten tired of my yapping and just plopped the box of found trinkets on the desk. I could tell she was anxious to get rid of me and back to her rag. She sorted through the contents and produced a necklace.

"Beads like this?" she asked.

"Yeah," I confirmed.

Then she got smart on me. "Most people call 'em *pearls*. Take a look and see if it's yours."

Yeah, most people call those fakes, but why argue? She had what I needed.

"Yeah, this is it," I told her. "Definitely her necklace. My wife'll be thrilled to get this back. It was a gift from her mother. A *wedding* gift. Thanks, Doll."

"Yeah, sure," she answered, already back nose deep in her rag.

I'm not sure she bought my act, but at that point I didn't care. I had what I needed to get to Irene Faye. And hopefully get something out of her.

CHAPTER TEN

I RECLAIMED my bucket and steered it down Wilshire towards Beverly Hills. I was getting famished, so I swung by Pink's again for a couple of dogs. I was getting to be a regular.

Going from West Hollywood into Beverly Hills feels like entering another country. I'm surprised they don't have a checkpoint and border patrol. Soon as you cross Doheny Drive, you're in the land of chauffeurs and caviar.

From there I steered up North Beverly. Eventually I found myself parked in the circular driveway of a giant, white mansion squeezed into the twists and turns of Benedict Canyon.

Don't know how they fit this place in there, but there it was. A three-story, Greco-Roman bungalow that would have made Nero proud.

The porch had four columns that hid the front door. When I walked through, I half expected to find a giant statue of Lincoln sitting behind it.

There was no time for gawking, though. It was time to sell my story again and hopefully chat up that blonde quail. I rang the bell and after a few minutes, the butler finally opened the portal.

He bought my bill of goods a lot easier than I thought. Guess it was the mention of Harper's party that did it. In minutes, "Jeeves" was trotting me through the museum that passed for a house.

"Mrs. Saltzman is out by the pool, Sir," he informed me.

I couldn't help but take it all in. More formal than Harper's beach shack, though I imagined his cutie's other digs down the street weren't too far off. "Wow, this is some palace," I chimed. "Derek must be doing pretty good for himself, eh?"

Thought I'd try to make polite conversation, but Jeeves wouldn't have it. This time he was the trained monkey.

"This way, Sir," he said as he ushered me out the back portal. We crossed a small patio to a watering hole that put Lake Michigan to shame.

"I thought you said pool, Jeeves," I piped. "I've seen lakes smaller than this."

Irene Faye swam over to the ladder. Jeeves gave a quick bow. "This gentleman is here to see you, Ma'am," he chirped dutifully.

"Thank you, Edward," she purred and after another head nod, off he went. I couldn't help but stand there and gawk while she climbed up out of the pool.

She looked even better wet than she did dry. She had on a two-piece that clung in all the right places. Like I said before, the statues in Greece had nothing on this dame.

"Would you mind handing me that towel?" she asked, nodding towards the lounge.

I picked my jaw up off the pavement and fetched like a dog goes for a stick. She used it to dry her hair while she gave me the up-and-down.

Of course, I did the same for her. And then some.

I could tell right off why she'd made it big in pictures. But what I couldn't figure was why she wasn't doing it anymore.

"What can I do for you?" she queried.

Time to sell my story again. "The name's Tom Miller, I was at Harper's party the other night, and found your necklace. You left before I was able to return it."

I procured the baubles from my pocket and held them up for her inspection. A woman like her would know right away they were fakes.

The little smile that crossed her beautiful kisser told me she did. She looked at me like a cat that's just found new prey. She wrapped the towel around her delicious frame. I liked it better on the chair.

"I didn't lose a necklace at Harper's party," she cooed. "But I do remember seeing you there. You're that reporter, aren't you? The hero."

That's right. You don't forget the trained monkey. The jig was up. But so what? I'd gotten to her and was armed with questions.

"Yeah," I confessed. "With the *LA Chronicle*. I'd like to get some information on Frank Kellman."

Her smile disappeared. "My husband has already spoken to the police several times. If he were to catch you here, he'd throw you out. He *hates* reporters."

I stepped closer anyways. Sure had the urge to do more than beat gums. "I didn't come here to talk to your husband, I came here to talk to *you*."

That got her attention. She gave me the up-and-down once more then sashayed over to the lounge. Tossed her towel aside and stretched out.

She was like a piece of art just waiting to be admired. The warm, afternoon sunlight glistened off of her wet, tan skin. Michelangelo could have toiled his whole life and never carved anything that even came close.

Yeah, I'll admit it. I was getting a little star-struck.

She threw on a pair of blinders and plucked a gasper from her purse. "All right," she cooed with that lioness grin. "But first, why don't you tell me what *you* know about Kellman?"

I pulled a lighter from my pocket and set her gasper on fire. "I know that he used to work for your husband. He's a convicted arsonist, been out of prison for six months, and he's the prime suspect for the arson case."

Her smile told me she was impressed. "I won't ask where you got that information."

She took a long haul off of her gasper and let the smoke drift up slowly. She was sizing me up, I could tell. Finally, she asked, "What makes you think I might know something that can help you?"

I could play that game, too. "I don't know, you tell me."

She took another long haul and held it a while before

letting it free. Then she spilled, "All I know is that he used to hang out a bar downtown."

"You wouldn't happen to know the name of this place, would you?" I queried.

"I think it was called O'Doule's," she informed me. "I haven't seen him since he went to prison. I can assure you, my husband has no plans to hire him back. There's really nothing more I can tell you."

She gave me the stare down just to make her point. Even with her glims hidden behind those blinders, I could read her expression loud and clear.

Whether she knew anything more or not, it didn't matter. That was all I was getting. I fished out a card and handed it to her. "If you do hear anything, call me."

She looked it over and gave me a hungry smile. "I may have to make up something."

I SHOWED myself out and steered my jalopy off to the nearest squawk box. I spilled the latest details to Jenkins. He was surprised I'd gotten in. Wasn't surprised that I hadn't got anything out of her.

Then it was back in my bucket for the drive downtown. I finally parked in front of O'Doule's gin mill a good while later.

I ankled it into the portal and took a good look around. The décor was all wood panels and liquor bottles. But that was about it. The place was deader than vaudeville.

A big, husky bartender with a crew cut and a demeanor to match barreled out of the back. He looked irritated that I'd bothered his beauty rest. "We don't open for another three hours," he barked in an Irish brogue so thick it could tenderize beef.

"That's okay," I told him. "I just want to ask a few questions. I'm looking for Frank Kellman. Hear this is where he used to hang out."

The gin slinger raised an eyebrow and lamped back at me with one eye shut. "I already talked to the cops. Who are *you*?"

So, Hap Underwood had already been there, too. He was more on the ball than he let on. No big surprise. But I still didn't like being one step behind.

I flashed him my credentials. "Name's Tom Miller. I'm with the *Chronicle*."

"Well," the bartender barked back. "I ain't seen Kellman since he went to the big house."

"You sure about that?" I asked as I passed him a sawbuck. He didn't even blink.

I got the feeling he knew more, but like with Irene Faye, that's all I was getting. No matter how much geetus I slipped his way.

I slipped my card across the bar. "You do hear anything, give me a call."

I ankled it back out the front portico, but hung close so I could hear inside. Like I figured, the juice slinger went straight to the horn.

"Yeah," he spilled. "Some guy was just in here asking about Frank Kellman."

He listened a second, then answered, "No, the cops was here last week. This guy was a reporter. With the *Chronicle*."

CHAPTER ELEVEN

WHO KNEW if I was making any headway? But I'd certainly made some waves. And sometimes, that's just as good.

I stepped outside O'Doule's and fumbled for a gasper. That's when I noticed the sweet little raven-haired trick waiting by my heap.

It was that dish from the *Tribune*, Flora Mason. She was hot on my heels like a dog after the mailman. If I didn't know any better, I'd think she was getting ideas. I know I was starting to get a few myself.

"So, I hear you were just up visiting Irene Faye," she purred.

"From who?" I asked. Though I knew she wasn't about to tell me. Not if she were even half her salts.

"I've got my sources, same as you," she shot back and gave me the up-and-down. "Light me up, will you?"

I plucked another gasper and offered it to her. She put it between her soft, red lips and leaned in close for a light. She stared at me with those beautiful green lamps and gave me a nice long peak in the process.

Clearly, she wasn't above using her feminine wiles to get information.

Truth be told, I wasn't above liking it.

"You actually used the old necklace gag?" she asked as she took a long drag and let the smoke drift out slowly.

"Can't believe she actually went for it."

Okay, I have to admit, that part took me by surprise. Had this dame been following me? If so, she was darn good at it. Clearly, there was a lot more going on between her cute little lobes than that gorgeous button.

"Got me in the door, didn't it?" I smirked. "What can I say? I'm a big fan."

If she'd tracked me that far, she must've known about the link between Kellman and Irene. Or did she even know *why* I was at O'Doule's?

She let out another long drag and gave me a smoldering nod towards the door. "How about you tell me all about it over a couple of drinks?"

"They don't open for a while yet," I told her. The disappointment obvious in my voice.

"Well, I'm sure we could find a bottle somewhere," she told me. "Your apartment, maybe?"

Got to admit the offer was tempting. *Real* tempting. But I knew she was just fishing. Hoping I'd get sloppy and cough up something worth printing.

"Sorry, Doll," I told her. "But my dance card is full this evening. Maybe some other time."

She leaned over the window as I climbed back into my jalopy. Gave me another long view of the real estate. The rolling curves of the Hollywood Hills are hard to pass up.

"If you get bored after curfew," she offered, "just give me a call."

Clearly she knew about Trudy, too.

NEXT DAY I was back in the office plotting my options on the arson story. No matter which way I looked at things, I was coming up bupkis. Right back where I started. Behind the eight-ball.

I'd weaseled my way into seeing Irene Faye. But the only thing I'd gotten there was an eyeful of gorgeous flesh. Not that I was complaining.

And put myself on the radar of that hot little raven-haired number from the *Tribune*. Not that I was complaining about that, either.

Had to be something I was missing.

I picked up Kellman's copy of *Tell-All Magazine* and flipped through the pages again. Like I said before, even in grainy newsprint, that Irene was one beautiful dish.

Kellman, on the other hand? Not even sure a mother could love that mug.

"Looking for a more appropriate publication for your talents?"

I looked back and found Gronchi staring over my shoulder. I was about to dish it right back when I got a better idea. Maybe she could be helpful for a change.

"Say, Gronchi, you're a dame," I told her.

"Nothing gets by you, does it?" she replied.

I decided to just let it go. "Tell me, why would a tomato like Irene Faye mess around with a guy like this Kellman?"

I was expecting another wisecrack. But instead she shook her little noggin and answered me honestly. "Some women just like the wrong kind of man."

Got the feeling there was a lot more to that story. Also got the feeling I'd be better off not asking.

Couldn't help but think of Trudy. I knew exactly what kind of man she preferred. But what I didn't know for sure was just how to live up to it. I still didn't know what I was doing with that sweet little dish. But the moment had gotten the better of me and I'd made a date with her. Far be it from me not to keep it.

Since drinking and dancing were out of the question, my options with Trudy were limited. So, it was dinner and a movie.

"Tell me something else, Gronchi," I asked. "Got my date with Trudy to-night. Where's a good place to go? She's a *real* nice girl, you know. Not the usual Hollywood type. You'd like her."

Gronchi scrunched her little nose and gave me a suspicious look. I made a halo over my head.

"Well, if you're telling the truth about her being a sweetheart, the Tick Tock Tea Room is perfect. If you're not, she'll never speak to you again."

Could have sworn she smiled on that last one.

WITH NO solid leads, I did what I always do. Beat the pavement. Still had two more possibilities that might pan out.

First stop was the shop where Kellman had bought his suit. It was a little one-room outfit in West Hollywood called Arzner's. Soon as I stepped inside I thought I was back in the Garment District.

Every inch of the joint was wall-to-wall clothing racks. Suits, shirts, hats, long coats, jackets, you name it. And in every color. I could barely find my way through the place. It was like a maze. And if for some reason you still couldn't find what you wanted, I guarantee you, it was "in the back."

Run by a tiny Russian Jew who looked like he'd just stepped out of Munchkinland. What little hair he had was parted in the middle and slicked down on both sides. His mouth was hidden by a big, bushy moustache and he wore those tiny little glasses that just sit on the nose.

Arzner was short on English but long on salesmanship. Every 30 seconds he'd offer me something else to buy. I was lucky to get out of there without a whole new wardrobe.

After I'd tried on about six or eight things, I finally got him to stop long enough to ask about Kellman. He didn't remember the name, but his face twisted in a little knot when I flashed Kellman's mug shot.

"Oh yes, I know him!" Arzner blurted. "He only buy one suit!"

I asked if he'd seen Kellman in the last six months. He was sure he hadn't.

"Never forget a customer!" Arzner proclaimed.

I wasn't about to doubt him. Half wondered if maybe he and Gronchi weren't related somehow.

But it made me wonder even more why Kellman hadn't gone back to get his things. He'd paid his debt. Why lay so low?

AFTER packing it up from Arzner's with a new lid and three new shirts in tow, I steered my jalopy all the way down Fairfax until I hit Culver City.

I pulled into King's Tropical Inn over on Washington Blvd. The place was big and white, typical Spanish-style architecture with red tile roof. Except for the giant dome in the middle that looked like it had been yanked straight off the the Capitol Building. Not exactly *tropical*.

It was early yet, since they didn't open till five. But most of the staff was there prepping for the dinner rush. I flashed my credentials and weaseled my way in.

The inside was a completely different story. The booths all looked like little bamboo huts with paper lamps. There was a giant floral arrangement in the middle. The whole ceiling was painted with clouds and stars. Diners were serenaded by tropical music and the occasional Crosby tune.

I was tempted to come back with Trudy just to see the place in all its glory. The prices weren't bad, either. Just like Old Lady Kratz said, for a buck twenty-five, you could get fried chicken, steak, or squab. Complete with sides, biscuit, ice cream, and coffee.

The Head Waiter was a middle-aged fellow, friendly but not too talkative. Wore the usual white shirt and apron. Which hung out like a sail around his midsection.

"Listen Pal," I told him. "I gotta ask. What's a squab?"

He went on to tell me that squab is "actually a young, domestic pigeon." In other words a fancy name for those flying park rats that steal your peanuts and deface statues. No thanks, Bub. I'll stick with steak and fried chicken.

When I asked about Kellman, I got the exact same story I'd gotten from Arzner. Just easier to understand and it didn't cost me anything. Used to be a regular, but they hadn't seen him since.

And that raven-haired doll had beaten me to both joints.

Back to square one. Again. I'd made better hay with Irene. What I really needed was a break. Something to go my way.

One thing still had me puzzled. This guy was doing one hell of a job keeping out of trouble. I was beginning to wonder if he was even in town.

CHAPTER TWELVE

I FOLLOWED Gronchi's advice and took Trudy to the Tick Tock Tea Room on North Cahuenga. Good thing, too, because it was perfect. A cozy little joint decorated with clocks (hence the name), run by a sweet, old Norwegian couple. Good food and easy on the wallet.

Towards one end was a four-sided, wooden tower with a fireplace on each side. And a cuckoo clock on every mantle. The wood panels on the walls gave the place a sturdy look. And the fresh flowers on every table added a soft touch.

I figured Gronchi was right. A sweet gal like Trudy would go for the down-home atmosphere, which she did. And it wasn't really big with the Hollywood crowd, which was fine by me. Plus, it was right off of Hollywood Blvd., close to both the Chinese and the Egyptian.

The place served three-course meals: we started with a basket of their famous Sticky Orange Rolls, then a fruit cocktail and cup of sherbet for appetizers, and finally entrees of meatloaf (hers) and fried chicken with gravy (mine).

Trudy was too stuffed for dessert, so I had the homemade lemon meringue pie to myself. Had to admit, everything about the place made me feel like home. Especially the company.

"You know," I told her, "all these clocks remind me of my grandma's house. She had a big collection. Books, too. Stacked books in the corner to make room for the clocks.

You should have heard the place every hour."

Trudy let out a chuckle. "I bet that was something!"

I pointed to a big, old timepiece on a nearby wall. "Oh yeah. She had a grandfather clock that looked just like that one. I used to steal the key and hide candy in the cabinet."

Trudy smiled back. "Were you close to your grandmother?"

This is where things got a little uncomfortable. I should have just said yes and been done with it. But every time I looked into those beautiful, blue peepers, I couldn't help but tell her the truth. "Wish I could say that I was," I replied.

That took her by surprise. Took me by surprise, too.

Trudy didn't have to say anything. She just took my mitt and looked back at me with those sweet baby blues.

"Unfortunately," I explained, "she was a drunk for most of her life. Hit the bottle first thing in the morning."

Trudy clutched my hand even tighter. I'm sure she didn't know what to say. It was all right. She didn't have to.

"Finally sobered up the last couple of years. One day I went over to see her, and we had a long talk about all the books we'd read. Best time I ever had with her. Then after I left, I just sat in my jalopy and wondered. *Where were you all my life?*"

"Oh, Tom, I'm so sorry," Trudy comforted me. Thought for a minute she was going to cry. If I didn't start bawling first.

"Hey kiddo, sorry for bringing you down," I apologized. "Don't know what made me tell that story."

She grabbed my mitt even tighter. Her skin was so soft it was like being held by an angel.

"You don't have to apologize," she assured me. "Yes, it was sad. But sweet. I'm just glad you trusted me enough to tell it."

AFTER DINNER, we trotted over to the Egyptian to catch one of the galloping tintypes. I was partial for the Cagney picture that was playing at the Chinese, but Trudy wanted something romantic.

If I wanted to get anywhere with this gal, I knew I had to give in. So, it was the romance flick at the Egyptian. Surrounded by dozens of sobbing torchbearers and their unlucky dates for the evening. Every one a poor sap just like me.

The Egyptian was built by a fellow named Sid Grauman. Same guy that built the Chinese. Only this one doesn't have footprints outside or the gawkers trying to spot a movie star. The outside looks like you're walking into the tomb of some Pharaoh.

Too bad they weren't playing a Mummy picture. This doll would've been in my arms the whole night.

Truth be told, the picture wasn't all that bad. Just not my cup of joe.

Afterwards, we climbed back in my jalopy and scooted back to her place. I played the gentleman, opened her car door, and escorted her up to the portico.

"Thank you for everything, Tom. I had a wonderful time," she gushed. Even in the moonlight, I could see stars in her eyes.

"Yeah, me too," I cooed. I slipped an arm around her small waist and moved in for a smooch.

She backed away real polite-like, hit me with that beautiful smile. "I'll see you to-morrow night?"

The message was clear. Not too fast, Bub. If you want this piece of cheesecake, you're gonna have to work for it.

All I could say was: "Yeah, sure, Baby."

She hit me with that smile again. Gave me a quick peck on the jowl and shut the portal behind her. It was still a good night out, despite the unhappy ending. But a kiss on the cheek was better than nothing.

Normally, I wouldn't have given this gal a second chance, but something told me I was starting to fall for her.

I ankled back to my jalopy then lit up a gasper and opened the door. About that time a Yellow went by. I tabbed the passenger out the corner of my optics. Even so, there was no mistake.

It was Irene Faye.

What was she doing driving by at this hour? And in a cab? There were no easy answers. Not headed back to Beverly Hills, that's for sure.

So, I jumped in my crate and gave chase. Made sure to keep back a safe distance. Didn't want her to know she was being followed.

CHAPTER THIRTEEN

I TAILED IRENE all the way downtown. Not in the hustle and bustle, mind you, by City Hall, Angels Flight, and Grand Central. But on the outskirts. Out by the river and railroad tracks. Where the trains come by every half hour.

Finally stopped outside a seedy dump called the Midnight Motel. It was one of those motor court stashes with a main office building in front and a long, rectangular parking lot. Sitting all around was a collection of one-room, white clapboard bungalows. Like a neighborhood street of tiny houses.

Behind the office was a pool. Though from the looks of things, I don't think anybody'd dipped a toe in it since before the war. It was dry as an open pit in the Sahara.

I parked across the street, then just sat in my jalopy and waited. Finally, she got out of the hack. It was Irene Faye, all right. Every inch a movie star. Even in a trash heap like that.

Thought she might go check in, but no dice. Instead, she went straight towards the bungalows.

I got out and followed. Kept my distance. Stuck to the shadows.

I ducked behind the parked jalopies to keep her in my optics. Watched her through the windows. I tabbed her scooting down to the far end. She stopped outside a corner hut, took a quick glance around. Then she went inside.

What was Irene doing out alone at night in a place like that? This was starting to look like just the break I needed.

I waited a few moments, went in for a closer look. If nothing else, I got the room number. Bungalow 16.

Tried to get a peek inside, but again, no dice. The curtains were pulled tighter than a fat man's underwear.

I stood at the portico and listened. Could hear movement, but no yapping. Looked like somebody was already there, waiting for her.

Kellman maybe? I had to be sure. But how?

There was no peeking inside without dusting that portal with my knuckles. And I'd have done it, too, if I hadn't already chatted her up at her place. Just yesterday, in fact. She would've tabbed me in a New York second.

Had to find another way.

I ankled it back down to the office, went inside, piped the Desk Clerk. He was a young Joe with a plump neck and nothing better to do.

He asked, "How can I help you, Sir?"

I leaned on the desk, flashed my credentials, and gave it to him straight up. "Wondering if you can tell me who's staying in Bungalow 16?"

He gave me a smarmy smile and shot back, "I'm sorry, Sir, but I can't give out that information."

So, that's how it's gonna be. This yokel wasn't as much of a chump as I thought. I realized this shack probably made more money telling who was *in* the rooms than they did renting them out.

I reached in my wallet and pulled out some persuasion. "Say, what's a room run these days? About ten a night?" I slipped a sawbuck across the desk.

"No," he said, never losing that grin. "I'm afraid it's a little more than that."

At least he was more appreciative than that bartender. I slipped him another skin. "What, you mean about twenty?"

That was the magic number. Chubby Neck reached for the guest book and flipped it open for me.

"Sir," he piped up, "if you would like to check in, you just need to sign here." He pointed to an empty line in the register.

I lamped the page and saw the goods right above his stubby finger: Bungalow 16, checked out by "George Matthews." No address or phone number.

I shook my noggin. "Shame. Room 16's already taken."

"So, you won't be staying, then?" He was clearly big on pretense.

"No thanks, pal. I'll pass."

"Please come again, Sir," he warbled and gave me a wink that made me wonder if he was light in the shoes.

I was halfway out the door before one more thought struck me. "Say, you haven't seen a raven-headed dish snooping around here, have you? She works for the *Tribune*."

"No Sir, can't say that I have," he replied.

Wasn't completely sure he wasn't feeding me a line of bull as I hadn't slipped him any more geetus. Could be she'd slipped him more to keep his yap shut.

But my gut was telling me I'd finally tread new ground on this story. And my gut was usually right as Abe Lincoln on a Sunday morning.

I stepped back out and glimmed in the direction of Bungalow 16. Didn't look like there'd been any movement while I was in the office.

George Matthews. Could have been an alias for Kellman. Didn't lamp it on his rap sheet, but that didn't mean he didn't pick a new one.

Or could have been a new sugar daddy for our Mrs. Faye. Dame seemed to get around. Either way, it was another trail.

There weren't too many jalopies parked there, so I pulled out my notepad and jotted down all the plates.

Kept one optic peeled on Bungalow 16. Just in case anyone amscrayed, I was ready to duck out.

I ankled it back to my crate and kept low so I could keep an eye on the place. Just my luck, there was a black and white cruising the neighborhood. I didn't want to draw attention to myself.

After he spotted me the second time, I put my bucket in gear and moved on.

CHAPTER FOURTEEN

EARLY the next morning, I was back for another peep. All the jalopies were gone except for two. I crept back down the drive for another gander at Bungalow 16. But the curtains were still shut tighter than a cellar door in a twister.

I ankled it back down to the office. Just my luck, Chubby Neck was working the desk again. He stood up straight when I ambled my tonnage through the portal.

"Back so soon?" he chirped.

I got straight to brass tacks, slipped a double-sawbuck across the counter. None too happy, either. This guy was costing me plenty and hadn't told me much of nothing. "Bungalow 16 check out yet?"

"Let me check and see," he clucked and flipped open the register. "Not likely. Mr. Matthews paid for the whole week. If he has left for the day, he should be back this evening."

Well, that was something. "What's this clown look like?" I asked.

Chubby Neck dallied his fingers like he was hitting me up for more geetus, but the topography of my map told him otherwise. So he went ahead and coughed it up anyways.

"Afraid I couldn't say. I wasn't working when he checked in."

Good thing I didn't pay up. Would have slugged him for that one. "Thanks, Pal," I told him. I went ahead and slipped him my card. He was happy to take it.

"Call my office if you see him come back, will you?"

FROM there it was straight back to the office. Passed Gronchi's desk on the way in. Just smiled and gave her the wave. She slanted up at me and gave out something that looked like an expression.

Curiosity, maybe? I let her stew and made a beeline for Jenkins' office. I filled him in on Irene and the motel. Asked if he had any skinny on this George Matthews fellow.

"George Matthews? Can't say I've ever heard of him. Of course, I'm not big into the Hollywood crowd. That party at Harper's was strictly business."

"I got the plates off all the buckets at the motel," I told him. "Maybe that'll get us an address."

"Good thinking, Miller. Just give Miss Gronchi the list. She'll have better luck tracing them."

Jenkins was right. Underwood and young Rigby were my only contacts at the LAPD. Rigby didn't have the pull I needed, no matter how much geetus I tossed his way. And Underwood wasn't about to spill on my account. Same reason.

"Thought I'd take a drive out to Chino first thing Monday morning and chat up Kellman's cellmate," I suggested. "See if he's got anything he's willing to cough up."

"Good idea, Miller. And good luck getting him to sing. Tell Gronchi to ring up the Warden. Let him know you're coming."

I finished filling in Jenkins, but left out any details regarding Trudy. No need to air that laundry again. I was just about to powder when he inquired anyways.

"So, how'd it go at the Tick Tock last night?" he asked.

Should have known. Tell Gronchi, tell the boss.

"Better grab on to something, Miller. Looks like you're getting dizzy for this dame," he ribbed.

I was barely back to my hovel when Gronchi was hovering over my desk with her little mitt out. "You have the list?" she asked.

"What list?"

"The license plate numbers," she clarified. "And I've already called the Warden at Chino. He's expecting you at 9:00 am."

"Looks like communication runs both ways around here," I observed. I pulled the list from my pad, tossed her the pages.

She lowered her cheaters, gave me the glare. "It's my job to know *everything* that goes on in this office."

Then she just stood there silently. Like she was waiting for a bus.

"Anything else you need, Baby?"

"That's *Miss Gronchi*, thank you. And it would be remiss of me to not inquire about your dinner engagement. If I may ask, was the restaurant satisfactory?"

"Just like I told you, Sweetheart..."

"Miss Gronchi," she interrupted.

"She's a nice gal. We're going out again to-night. Still time to make the front page?"

She let out a barely audible "hmph" of surprise, readjusted her cheaters. "Very good then." She turned on her little heel and swayed back to her desk.

That out of the way, it was time to get some work done. Didn't know why everybody was so intrigued by my business. Certainly wasn't that way back East.

I grabbed the directory out of my desk and flipped to M. There were 42 names listed under "Matthews, George." Or some variation thereof.

Wish'd the guy been named "Gaucho Rodriguez" or something with a little more zip to it. Would've been much easier to track down. Of course, there was no guarantee the fellow was even a local. Could just as likely been from out of town.

I spent the rest of the day ringing every number, posing as a private dick or a vacuum salesman, asking about Irene.

Got more than a few hang-ups and, I'm sure, several joes in Dutch with their wives. All of it led to the exact same place.

Just another big, fat dead end.

TOOK a break from chasing my tail to ankle down to the local hash house, Veda's Cafe. It was one of those corner shops with a long bar next to the kitchen and a booth with Formica tables by every window.

You know what they say about real estate. Location, location, location. This joint had the good fortune of being only two blocks from the office. That, a good cup of joe and a decent slice of pie guaranteed it a steady stream of customers.

I'd just taken a bite of my burger when, lo and behold, Hap Underwood sat down across from me. He'd barely hit the leather before the waitress was right behind him with a cup of swill and his own slice of cherry tart.

"What'dya know good, Tom?" he asked, making himself comfortable.

"Still looking to fit me for a pair of nippers?" I queried.

"Forget that," he told me. "I was just trying to size you up. So, you making any headway on your story?"

"Maybe, you looking to make a trade?" I grinned. "Or just want me to do your job?"

He leaned back and offered me a wide smile. "You got it all wrong, Miller. This isn't like back East out here. We're more friendly. You scratch my back, I scratch yours."

"Oh, we do the same thing back East," I informed him. "Only we don't do it out of friendship." I mean, they might call it friendship, but the truth is a little more sinister.

"But I'll play along," I replied. "What do you want to know?"

"For starters," Hap replied, "you can tell me about your visit with Irene Faye. What was that all about?"

Well, that was an eye-opener. Suddenly everyone wants to know. Looked like I had a leg up on more than just Flora Mason.

"Word sure gets around, huh?" I had to ask.

"What can I say?" he explained. "It's a small town. Company town at that."

"So I've noticed."

I wasn't against helping the cops if I had something I thought they could use. But at this point, all I had were a bunch of wild guesses and maybes.

Only I wasn't about to tell him that.

"Tell you what," I offered. "I'm not at liberty to share anything just yet. But when the time comes I get something real solid, you'll be the first to know."

"Can't ask for anything more than that," Hap replied.

Nothing like having the law on your side. Never know when it might come in handy.

CHAPTER FIFTEEN

WHEN IT got close to final bell, I made for the jalopy and steered back to the motel. Luckily, it was only a ten minute scoot from the office. Almost a straight shot down 7th.

Didn't bother with Chubby Neck. Didn't have the geetus to spare. There weren't any new cars and the curtains on Bungalow 16 hadn't budged an inch.

Whoever this guy was, he was hard to pin down.

I hung around for as long as I could, but I had another date with Trudy. That's when it dawned on me. She knew who all the Hollywood types were. Maybe she could steer me on the right path.

I climbed in my bucket, hightailed it over to West Hollywood. After making nice with the landlady and promising to have her back before curfew, we shuffled back to the Tick Tock Tea Room. It had worked wonders the first time around. Why not a second go?

"LISTEN BABY," I told her. "You might be able to give me the dope on something. You ever hear of anybody in the business named George Matthews? Maybe a friend of Irene Faye's?"

She glimmed me with surprise all over her beautiful map. "What's this about?" She folded her napkin neatly.

"Story I'm following," I explained. "Can't say more about it now, but I'll fill you in later. Ever hear of the guy?"

She scrunched up her little nose, let it have a run through her pretty noggin. "No, I don't think so. Wish I did. I've never helped run down a story before. And it involves Irene Faye? Sounds like it could be big."

She folded her napkin again.

"Could be. You tab anything later, drop me a dime, okay?"

"Of course," she said, then creased her napkin once more.

"Something eating you, Baby? I don't think that napkin can take much more."

Her map went red as a cherry, did a stare down with the floor. "Yes, there's something I wanted to tell you."

I could only imagine what had gotten her dimples in a knot. "Spill it, Doll. It's okay," I reassured her.

"Well, I'm afraid I haven't been *completely* honest with you," she confessed. "After you were so forthcoming, telling me all about your grandmother, I just feel terrible."

"Hey, it can't be that bad, Baby."

"The truth is, I lied about the movie last night. I didn't want to see that romance picture. I really wanted to see the Cagney picture at Grauman's. To be perfectly honest, I can't stand women's pictures. I really love *action* movies."

"Is that it?" I chuckled. Could have knocked me over with a dirty sock. And just when I thought this little cutie was as white bread as they come.

"Yes," she said, and buried her face in her pretty little hands.

I reached across the table, lifted her chin. "Why the waterworks, Doll?"

"I was just afraid you wouldn't think it was very ladylike of me."

"Listen, Baby, if you were any more woman, you'd be Venus and Aphrodite all rolled into one. You put 'em all to shame, Sweetheart."

"You really think so?" she asked.

"I know so, Baby."

It was still early yet, and I wasn't quite ready to take her home. I suggested we head over to Griffith Park to look at the stars. Up to the Observatory.

Thought for sure she'd shoot me down on that one. But truth be told, she was game for the idea. Second surprise of the night.

Have to admit, this gal was a real head-scratcher. Talk about a load of contradictions.

Not the kind of girl who drinks or smokes, but she crashed a Hollywood party. Doesn't go to clubs, but likes action pictures. Looks like an angel, but she's built for sin. Sweet as they come, but sweet on a guy like me.

Go figure.

AFTER dinner, we took a drive up Western Canyon Road to Griffith Observatory. Despite all the hairpin turns, it was still only a twenty minute jaunt. Seemed like a lot of young lovers had the same idea.

Instead of going inside to take in the show, we took the circular stairs on the left up to the East Observation Terrace. The sun was going down and it was just getting dark. The real stars overhead made for better backdrop anyways.

Not too far in the distance you could see all the lights of downtown LA. Couldn't help but think that one of those thousands of tiny glimmers was Jenkins back at the office. Burning the midnight oil, as usual.

We followed the Promenade Walkway around the Planetarium dome. The path was pretty narrow and it was a bit of a snug fit. Made our way to the West Terrace on the other side.

Trudy pointed me to look out towards the parking lot. Actually, she was directing my gaze off to the left. Towards the Hollywood hills directly behind us.

"Look up at the top," she told me, "you can see the Hollywoodland Sign."

I'd never seen it so close before. What was left of it anyways. The H had fallen over a few years earlier and the rest wasn't in great shape either. None of the 4000 bulbs were lit anymore. Even so, I still felt sorry for the poor fellow who's job it'd been to change them.

Trudy explained that the Sign was built for some real estate deal that never paid off. The boys behind it wanted to make a big splash. So they built the Sign to get people's attention. A giant billboard you could see for miles.

The letters used to light up in a pattern. First in

sections: HOLLY. WOOD. LAND. Then the whole thing: HOLLYWOODLAND.

But it wasn't built to last. So by this point, it had long been dark and was falling apart. Just a sad reminder of times past. Like a lot of things in Tinsel Town these days. Especially the Boulevard.

Me? I'd rather gaze at the real heavens. Way up there in the skies above. It was the perfect night for it. Sky was bright, the stars were out, and there was just a tiny chill in the air.

I put my coat around her and we looked up at the cosmos. I tell you, it was the kind of night that inspires a fellow to wax poetic when he's with a beautiful dish.

The moon was so big it looked like you could just reach up and touch it.

"Listen, Trudy," I stumbled for just what to say. For a guy who makes his living as a wordsmith, my stamp-licker wasn't exactly cooperating.

"I hope you don't mind me saying," I blathered, "but you're the first girl I've ever met that I feel totally at ease with. I guess because you seem so honest, I don't have to impress you."

"You just did," she smiled back and flashed those beautiful peepers.

"You know, it's a beautiful night out," I told her and pointed up at the sky. "Kind of night where a fellow just wants to reach out and kiss the girl he's with. If she won't back away."

"I'm sorry about that," she explained. "I've just been afraid."

"Afraid of what?" I had to ask.

"Of falling in love," she told me, then looked away, embarrassed.

Again I fished for just the right words. "What's there to be afraid of, Baby?"

It was then or never. I took her by the dainty wing and pulled her closer. Only this time she didn't back off.

I stared into those soft blue peepers until I just couldn't stand it any longer. That's when I took her in my arms and kissed her. Ever so softly.

"See, that wasn't so bad, was it?" I asked.

She blushed and turned away. Then she looked back at me with a playful grin. "Hmmm, I don't know. Let me try it again."

We locked lips once more and my coat fell right on the ground. Only neither one of us noticed.

Or cared.

CHAPTER SIXTEEN

MONDAY MORNING I was back in my jalopy. Still breathing the fresh air of Cloud Nine. Trudy and I ended up making a weekend of it. All of which included church on Sunday morning and an afternoon picnic by the lake in Echo Park.

Nothing but sunshine and roses. All of which made the near hour-long drive east past Pamona, out to Chino State Prison, that much easier.

Soon as I got there, I stopped in and had a nice little chat with the Warden. His office looked like a library, with a big mahogany desk and dark, wooden shelves all chock full of hardbacks.

With his leather chair, humidor, and his own personal stash of gin in the corner, it was clearly the lap of luxury. Especially compared to the concrete prison walls that surrounded it.

A paradise in the middle of purgatory.

He was a bookish-looking fellow with black-rimmed cheaters and hair slicked down like he'd just stepped out of the barbershop. For all I knew, he might've.

After we'd made do with the niceties, I quizzed him for some background details. Wanted to know just how to push a certain inmate's buttons.

Afterwards, a screw led me down to one of the interrogation rooms. Instead of the usual trip to Visitation,

Gronchi'd gotten him to give me a little more free reign. Hell of a gal, that Gronchi. Gonna make some lucky guy a real good wife one day.

The interrogation room was as bare bones as they come. Concrete with a heavy door, a large wooden table with a ring bolted in the middle, and two metal chairs.

The only attempts at decoration were the scratches on the furniture. And the blood stains on the wall.

Kellman's former cellmate was a guy named Arnold Lubin. Wiry little hombre, red hair, early 30s, kept a match tucked in one ear. Couldn't have been more than five foot on a good day. With lifts.

Got the distinct impression that, had the good Lord blessed him with another half foot, he'd might've chosen a better path in life.

Instead he was a car thief. Repeat offender. Every time he'd completed a stretch, he'd be back in the hoosegow inside of six months.

Soon as the Screw brought him in, he plopped down in the chair across from me and propped his little feet up on the table. I'd barely gotten out two syllables before he immediately tipped me to the score.

"Lookit," he informed me, "I ain't telling you nothing. I already talked to that shamus and I didn't tell him nothing, neither. Or that doll reporter. If *she* didn't get anywhere, *you* don't stand a chance."

I didn't have to ask the name. Or the hair color. I knew exactly who he meant. One day, this gal was going to be trouble. I was sure of it. Was only a matter of *when*.

Actually, he'd just done me a huge favor. My time was limited. And he'd just saved me a good deal of it letting me know where I stood.

"A real dish, that one," he continued. "Pretty dangerous for a doll like that to come out here. She's got real spunk, for sure. I'll be dreaming about her for weeks."

"Well, I guess you'll be heading back to your cell then?" I asked.

"No, you got me for twenty minutes," he scoffed. "We can talk about anything else. Pick a topic."

Good thing I came prepared. I was sure Underwood had

dangled the possibility of a reduced sentence. And Flora Mason had relied on her feminine charms. But I had other ideas. Normal means of persuasion didn't work in a place like this.

I pulled a deck out of my coat pocket, tapped the end, and fingered a gasper. Then I watched his eyes as I set the deck on the table and lit up.

Yeah, just like I thought.

I could play this game. And play it darn good, too. There's two things that jail rats want. Flora Mason was one, but she was out of reach. I had the other. And in ample supply.

I blew a fresh cloud in his direction. "So, Lubin, who do you like for the playoffs?"

He quickly scoffed, "The Yankees! Who else? Trust me, they got it in the bag."

"I don't know," I shook my noggin as I blew another cloud his way. "I'm thinking the Dodgers look pretty good, too. You know they got that colored player, Robinson, on the field this year."

I pulled another deck from my coat. Set it right on top of the first one. It did not go unnoticed.

"I don't care if the Dodgers got Babe Ruth himself," he scoffed again. "Believe me, the Yankees are going all the way to the Series! All the way, baby!"

"Think we'll ever get a pro team out here?" I pondered.

Lubin could only shrug, "Maybe one day. Who knows? Doubt any of these Nancy boy Hollywood types are any good at cracking a bat."

Couldn't disagree with that one. I added another deck to the pile. Then a fourth. Figured by that point I'd earned a dig.

"Okay, I gotta ask you one thing," I plied. "What's it like sharing a cell with a guy who's been keeping time with Irene Faye?"

He scoffed again. "That Kellman's a liar. Used to brag all the time about working for her. Swore up and down they was drinking out of the same bottle. But he was full of it, I tell you."

I blew another cloud in his direction. He sniffed it up like Grandma's fresh apple pie.

"I don't know," I told him. "They looked pretty chummy in *Tell-All Magazine*."

"Don't believe everything you read in those rags," he retorted. "He might've driven her around, but I *guarantee* you he never put a hand on that doll."

Now that I'd gotten him on topic, it was time to lower the boom. I snuffed out my gasper. Then I picked up a deck from the table and stuck it back in my pocket.

Lubin pretended not to notice. Or at least, like he didn't care.

That is until I pocketed another one.

"Say, where you going with those?" he asked. "I thought we was here to make a deal?"

I glanced at my watch. "Time's almost up, Lubin. And you already said you didn't want to gab about Kellman. Figured you'd already spilled enough."

I took away another deck.

He sat there anxiously for a second. Then motioned towards my coat pocket.

That's when he finally broke. "Okay, how about you put all them packs back on the table, huh?"

"And then what?" I asked him as I fingered the last one.

"Yeah, yeah," he beckoned, "I'll give you the whole scoop. Scout's honor."

I stuck it back in my pocket. That's when he started singing like Sinatra.

"All right, I'll tell you what he said. I'll tell you everything. Kellman says he was framed. Said her husband caught the two of them together one night. Said Saltzman's the real jealous type. Frank never lit that house up. Said it was just a big frame job to get back at him. Kellman said when he got out, he was going to burn Saltzman's big old house down. Then run off with Irene Faye."

So Kellman had it out for Saltzman. And was head over heels for the Mrs. Couldn't say as I blamed him. The picture was finally starting to come into focus. But not all of it.

"Tell me something," I asked and put a deck back on the table. "If that's Kellman's big plan, why hasn't he done it? Instead he's just been torching lots of other places."

Lubin just scratched his cranium on that one. "Search

me. But I can tell you one thing for sure, though. Kellman don't like anybody snooping in his business. I wouldn't get too close if I were you."

Lubin pointed out the scar just below his eye. "Opened one of his letters by mistake."

"Just one more question," I told him as I got up and unloaded another deck. "You ever hear the name George Matthews?"

"Yeah, sure," Lubin replied. "There's at least three guys in there with that name."

"Kellman ever mention it?" I asked. "Use it as an alias?"

"Maybe," Lubin replied. "Couldn't say for sure."

I emptied my pockets back out on the table. Tossed him an extra one for his troubles.

I'D JUST gotten back to my apartment stash later that evening, ready to call it a night. That's when I found a small, brown envelope somebody'd slid under the portal.

At first I didn't pay it any mind. Just picked it up and tossed it in with the rest of the bills. Figured Old Man Bellem had just gotten lazy on prying me for the rent.

But then it struck me.

It was a little thick for a bill. There was something small and square-shaped inside. So I tore it open and emptied the contents.

It was a green matchbook. From the Tick Tock Tea Room.

At first, I just shrugged it off. But then it hit me.

It was a message.

Trudy!

CHAPTER SEVENTEEN

I JUMPED back in my bucket and had all four tires squealing before I even made it out of the driveway. I hightailed it back to West Hollywood so fast it was a wonder I didn't have half the cops in LA hot on my keister. But I wasn't about to stop for any red lights. High on a pole or flashing on top of a car.

Soon as I rounded the corner outside Trudy's boarding house I slammed on the brakes. And darn near hit a fire truck.

The place was surrounded by hose jockeys and beautiful gals watching from the street. All outside in their bathrobes and negligee.

A giant plume of smoke billowed out the back. Like the Hebrews were crossing the Red Sea. But the house was still in one piece. Looked like the boys in raincoats had gotten there just in time.

I pushed my way through the crowd looking for Trudy. Passed by one gorgeous dish after another. But not the one I wanted.

There was no sign of her. That's when I started to panic.

Fortunately, I managed to run into the Fair Anita. The little blonde cutie who'd ditched her that night at the party. "You seen Trudy?" I asked.

"No!" she cried.

I was just about to dash inside when Chief Baker came

out waving his arms. Same guy who tried to stop me from my previous bit of heroics. He was followed by most of his crew. All rolling up their hoses.

"Calm down, just calm down," he instructed. "Everything's okay. Just a grease fire. Lot of smoke, but nothing serious. It's going to be all right."

"A grease fire?" everyone shouted in surprise. "What on earth?"

"That's right," Chief Baker confirmed. "Someone left a pan burning in the kitchen. It'll be okay once all the smoke clears out. You little gals just need to be more careful next time."

We let out a sigh of relief. But it didn't last long. There was still no sign of Trudy.

I was about to barrel into the house anyways when I spotted her coming up the block. She'd just gotten off the Red Car. Fit as an angel. Dressed in her little white waitress uniform.

Her optics were big as saucers. Locked on all the fire trucks and everyone standing outside. "What on earth happened?" she exclaimed. "Tom, what are you doing here?"

I couldn't answer. I just grabbed her in my arms and held her tight. I hadn't been this scared since the war.

Finally, I let her go long enough to breathe. And get in a few questions of my own. "Where you been, Baby? I was worried sick!"

"I had to do a double shift at work," she explained. "One of the girls called in sick. I couldn't believe it when I saw all this."

After the Fair Anita and I told her what happened, I offered to take them both to a hotel for the night. Truth be told, I was still a little worried about the message I'd gotten just an hour before. Only I kept that part to myself. She'd already had enough of a jolt for one night.

"Oh, Tom, you don't have to do that," she protested.

"Look," I explained, "with all that smoke, you don't want to go back in there till to-morrow at least. It's either that or you're staying at my place. And I know you don't want to do that."

She couldn't argue with me there.

THE CITY BURNS AT NIGHT

Only problem was, I didn't know too many hotels in the area. I wasn't about to take them downtown, especially not to the Midnight Motel.

Only other places I knew were the Roosevelt and the Hotel Hollywood, both of which were on the Boulevard, right by the Chinese. And a little heavy for my wallet.

Luckily, the Fair Anita knew of the perfect digs just a short scoot away. I got the feeling she'd been there a few times before.

FIRST THING the next morning, I was back at their rented digs bright and early. Wanted to check on Trudy and make sure she was still safe and sound. All looked good. No flashing lights or fire trucks. Just peace and quiet. Exactly what I wanted to see.

I tricked it up to her room and dusted the hatch a few times. Not too loud, but enough to be heard.

Was just about to leave when Trudy answered. She was in her bathrobe and just cracked the portal enough to talk. I could barely see her, but one thing was for sure. Even straight out of bed, she was still beautiful as could be.

"Tom?" she reacted with surprise. "What are you doing here?"

"Sorry to wake you, Sweetheart," I confessed, "but I just wanted to make sure you two gals are still safe."

She smiled back at me. "Yes, we're just fine here. All thanks to you."

"Good, good," I told her. I stumbled for something else to say. Anything other than the real reason I was there. But I just came up empty-handed.

"You gals need a ride anywhere?" I finally asked.

"Tom, really," she insisted, "you've done enough. We're fine. We'll just take the Red Car."

"Yeah, of course," I replied. "But you need anything, you just call. I'll be right over."

"Well, right now I really need some more beauty rest. See you soon?"

"Look," I stopped her, my nerves starting to show. "I was just wondering if maybe you might want to stay here a few more nights? Maybe give the place a little more time to air out?"

She gave me a puzzled look. "Tom, is there something you're not telling me?"

"No, Baby," I assured her. "It's just that little episode last night gave me the chills. I worry about you, Doll."

She smiled back again. "I like that you do. But we're just fine here, so don't worry anymore. Now close your eyes."

Wasn't sure what that was all about, but I did as instructed. She yanked the door open further, gave me a quick smooch, and then shut it just as fast.

If I hadn't needed to beat tracks downtown, I would've definitely stuck around for more.

A HALF-HOUR LATER I was back at my desk. Fumbling the pack of matches from the Tick Tock between my digits. I'd been hot on Kellman's trail for days. And now it looked like he was on *mine*.

That part didn't bother me. Just the opposite, actually. Told me I was clawing in the right direction.

There was one thing that did nibble on my brisket. Maybe the grease fire had just been a coincidence. I could buy that one, sure. But the matchbook had clearly been a warning. And proof that I was on the right track.

I'd just wished Trudy wasn't standing in the crossfire.

About that time, Gronchi sidled up and plopped a stack of papers on my desk. "What's all this?" I asked.

"Finished running all those plates for you," she explained. "Sorry to interrupt your day dreaming with bad news, but none of them belong to anybody named George Matthews. Or Frank Kellman. Or anyone connected to Kellman."

What'dya know? Another dead end. This Kellman was really good at covering his tracks.

"Got a message for you, too," she added and handed me a slip of paper.

Meet me at my place right away. Come around to back. It was signed, "Irene."

"What's that all about?" she asked.

"Just following the story," I told her.

"Yeah, sure," she replied. And threw me a disapproving look.

CHAPTER EIGHTEEN

I DIDN'T waste any time hauling my bucket across town to Beverly Hills. Only this time there was no one to greet me. No butler or anybody. And the door was locked. So I did as instructed and just went around to the back. That's where I found her.

Swimming at the far end of the pool.

She called out. "I see you got my message. I hope you didn't have any trouble finding your way in. I gave the servants the day off."

"It was no trouble," I assured her. "Figured you'd be out here. That's where rich folks usually spend their time."

"I wasn't always rich," she informed me. "I just married well. The fact is, most of the people in this town came from nothing."

She swam in my direction. That's when I noticed her distinct *lack* of swimwear. Nothing except a bathing cap.

I cleared my throat and adjusted my lid. This doll was doing her best to rattle me. And she was doing a pretty darn good job of it, too.

But I wasn't about to let on. Everything was jake as far as she was concerned.

"So, what'd you want to see me for?" I asked.

She reached the side where I was standing and lowered her blinders. Gave me a real disapproving look. "Well, I was certainly anxious to see what your reaction would be," she chastised. "But I didn't think you'd just ignore me altogether."

She was definitely playing me. And I wasn't above letting her. "You're a married woman," I told her.

"Don't let that stop you," she cooed. "Please, help me out, will you?"

I glanced around then glimmed the table and umbrella. Her robe was laying across the lounge chair. "Wouldn't you rather put something on first?"

"What, and get it all wet?" she asked. "Come on, be a gentleman and help me out." Got to give her credit. This doll didn't give up easy.

I reached over and took her by the wing. She took her own sweet time climbing up the ladder. I was careful to avert my optics. But not too much.

"Such a darling, thank you," she offered.

I turned my back as she made her way over to the chair. Once again, she took her own sweet time. She pulled off her bathing cap and fluffed her beautiful blonde tresses. Then she finally put on her robe and stretched out on the chair. "It's safe to look now," she informed me.

I loosened my tie and turned around. "What was it you wanted to tell me?"

"Please, sit down," she insisted as she lit up a gasper. "These lounge chairs are more comfortable than they look."

"Yeah, sure," I agreed.

I'd just plopped down across from her when this older fellow in a short-sleeve button-down and ascot barreled up. He gave me the stink-eye like I'd just grabbed the last slice of cake from the fridge. His map was all red and he was ready to spit fire.

Good thing he hadn't walked up a minute earlier.

"Darling!" he demanded. "Who is this man?"

Irene made quick work of the introductions. "Derek, this is Tom Miller. He's a reporter for the *Chronicle*. Mr. Miller, this is my husband, Derek Saltzman."

So, this was Saltzman, I thought as I sized him up. I'd been wanting to get a load of this mug ever since that night at Harper's party.

He was older than I expected. Had Irene by a good ten

years. Maybe more. He was handsome enough, with a dimpled chin and small moustache. But with his slicked hair and soft hands, I could tell he'd never done an honest day's work.

But the part that threw me was the decidedly British twang. Not the fake one you hear all the time in the galloping tintypes. No, this was the real deal. Old Derek sounded like he'd just quaffed down a plate of bangers and mash. All while sitting under the Union Jack and humming *God Save the King*.

Now, I'd known quite a few limeys in my time. Even fought the Nazis with a few who'll be my brothers till the day I cash in my chips. But I never expected to meet a limey with a Jewish moniker. Especially not in a town where they run just about everything.

Saltzman, for his part, was still spitting vinegar. "I think you'd better leave!"

That's when Irene suddenly changed her tune. "Actually, Darling. I was just about to throw him out."

"See to it that you do," he sneered. But before he made tracks, there was something I had to ask.

"That's an interesting accent you have, Mr. Saltzman. I would have pictured you being from back East."

Old Derek was suddenly short on words. He just looked at me with a blank expression on his visage. We just stood there with the dead silence hanging like a ton of bricks.

It was Irene who broke the ice. "Actually, my husband is second-generation Hollywood. He was schooled in Europe."

I guessed Old Derek wasn't used to being challenged. "Thank you, Darling," he told her.

Then just before he stormed off, he turned his pointed nose back up at me and sneered, "Mr. Miller."

I waited until Derek was out of sight before making my inquiries. "If you don't mind my asking, what's your husband doing here? Thought you two were on the outs."

She stared back at the house like she could spit nails. "He just drops by from time to time to make sure I'm behaving myself. He still likes to keep close tabs on me."

Yeah, well I couldn't exactly blame him on that front.

"Let me walk you to the front gate," she told me. "He'll

watch us to make sure you leave."

With all the melodrama, I'd almost forgotten why I came in the first place. Wasn't sure if she was playing me again. Or really was on the up-and-up. After we'd rounded the house, I implored her to come clean. "Say, what was it you wanted to tell me? Or are you just yanking my chain?"

She looked back at me like I'd just slapped her mother. "No, Tom. This is serious! Dead serious."

Had to admit she was mighty convincing. She looked back towards the pool to make sure we were out of earshot. Then she leaned in close and whispered.

"I received a very distressing phone call this morning. It was a man. He didn't say who he was, but I *know* it was Kellman. He said he was coming back for me."

Obviously, there was something more going on. Sounded to me like the gossip rags had it right all along. I had to make sure. "What, were you two really keeping time together?"

"I've never told anyone this before, but I feel I can trust you," she clutched my arm.

"You should never trust a reporter," I warned her.

"I learned that lesson a long time ago. But, you strike me as different. Not at all like those other bloodhounds."

That's when she came clean and spilled all the goods. "Anyway, this was after I found out about my husband. We were already separated. The affair was all my fault. I was all alone here. I was the one who initiated it. It was only later that I found out about Kellman's criminal past."

"So, it's not like you were running around behind Saltzman's back?" I asked.

"Exactly," she agreed. "I didn't think it would matter to him. But I was *wrong*. He hired some men to beat up Kellman. And then he framed him for *arson*."

She sure knew how to pick a winner. Between Kellman and Saltzman, sounded like she had a bad habit of hooking up with the wrong guys. I could see the look of fear in her eyes.

"Now that Kellman's out of prison, I'm afraid he'll come back for revenge," she worried. "He blames me for what Derek did. I can't say that I fault him. He may try to kill me. Or worse. And if my husband finds out about any of this, heaven knows what he'll do."

"So I've heard," I told her.

I knew this doll was an actress, but she had to be a darn good one to fake a performance like that. Cued the briny waterworks and everything.

"I'm so afraid, and I don't have anyone to turn to."

She just required a little reassurance. "Take it easy, Doll," I told her. "I'll help the cops nab Kellman. Then you won't have a thing to worry about."

That was all she needed to hear. "Somehow, you've just made me feel very safe."

By that time we'd reached the front turnstile. Where my jalopy was hitched out on the street. She glanced up towards the house again, worried that Derek might still be watching.

"I tell you what," she offered, "there's a party I'm attending to-morrow night at the Grove. I'd really appreciate it if you'd come."

There was still a part of me that wondered if she wasn't playing me for a dope. But every time I looked at this dame, there was a bigger part of me that didn't exactly care.

"Uh, okay," I told her. "Sure."

"Well then, I'll look forward to seeing you there," she smiled. Was just about to climb back into my jalopy when she added one more detail.

"Oh, and *do* come alone."

IT WAS dark when I made it back to my apartment stash. The only lights were from the street lamps, doorways, and scattered windows here and there. I'd just parked my bucket when one light in particular grabbed my attention. It was right across the street and the brightest of all.

Don't know how I hadn't noticed it before. But there it was in all its blazing glory. Right there on the marquis of that old movie house across from my hovel.

IRENE FAYE in
THE WOMAN IN QUESTION

It was one of her pictures. I think it'd come out during the war. Back in the *good old days* before Old Derek and the Studio had written her off. The perfect chance to see what I'd been missing.

I checked my watch.

I didn't even bother making a stop in my igloo. I just ankled it across the boulevard and bought a ticket from the little brown-eyed cutie working the box office. And took the opportunity to dig for a little info. "Say Sweetheart, which way is it to the Grove?

She looked at me like I was an idiot. Which wasn't too far from the truth. "The Cocoanut Grove? It's right down on Wilshire, inside the Ambassador."

"Thanks, Doll, for helping a fellow out," I told her. "Afraid I'm a little new in town. You've been a real peach."

She just shrugged and shook her head in disbelief. Hey, right with you, Sweetheart.

With a soda pop and barrel of popped kernels in hand, I grabbed my seat towards the back, center row. No sooner had I made myself comfortable, the lights went down.

The theater was only half full, if that. I could only imagine she'd commanded bigger crowds just a few years earlier.

Trudy'd told me that after Irene's fallout with Old Derek, the Studio wouldn't touch her. From what I could see, it looked like the public felt the same way.

After a comedy short, a newsreel, and a couple of coming attractions, I was getting impatient. Thankfully, it wasn't much longer before we finally got to the feature presentation.

The picture was about a fellow named Johnny. Down on his luck and drinking his way through Mexico. He gets a job working at a club run by Nick, a hot-tempered American gangster. The only kind.

Enter Irene. She played the gangster's moll, Laurel. A luscious blonde with smoldering eyes and curves in all the right places. Naturally, the poor sap falls for her. And falls hard.

Laurel wants out. She's tired of Nick telling her what to do. And getting slapped around for her troubles. She wants to hightail it back to the States. Preferably with a suitcase full of Nick's cash in tow.

Plus she wants Nick dead.

Enter Johnny.

In person, Irene was really something. I'd already gotten a taste of that. But seeing her there, up on that big screen, in all her glory? Well that was something else.

I could see where any guy would fall for her. Head over heels. She'd still be there in his grey matter long after the lights went up. And then he'd dream about her night after night when he got home.

She was a siren. A goddess. The kind of dame that drives a fellow bonkers.

The kind of dame that a fella would kill for.

CHAPTER NINETEEN

NEXT NIGHT I steered my bucket down Wilshire and found myself parked outside the Ambassador Hotel. It was a big, sprawling castle that took up almost the whole block. Grade A digs back in its day, and for a lot of decades after.

The place was built back in 21, when Wilshire stretched through the middle of nowhere and housing was in short supply for all the Hollywood types moving into town. Trudy told me you could look out the window back then and see all the way to the Pacific. Not sure I buy it, but it makes for a good story.

Directly across the street was the world famous Brown Derby. Still couldn't get over why anyone would build a restaurant in the shape of a hat. But that's Hollywood for you. Everything built for show and then some.

Took the side entrance of the hotel (which was actually the primary portal) off the parking lot and worked my way past all the ground floor shops. Found a set of stairs that took me up to the lobby level and the famous Cocoanut Grove.

Back then, the Grove was the place to see and be seen. Everybody who was anybody went there. Along with everybody who *wanted* to be somebody. And all the camera boys who wanted to make a quick buck snapping pictures of the whole lot.

The club itself was the biggest I'd ever seen. Unlike New

York, LA's got a lot of space. And they put it to good use at the Grove. The wide stage fit a full orchestra (usually Glenn Miller or Tommy Dorsey). Off the dance floor was a sea of tables. Enough to fit the whole population of Burbank and Glendale combined.

Naturally, the place had a tropical theme. Very popular in those days. The whole club was decorated with fake palm trees. But unlike King's Tropical Inn, these were top notch. They'd come off the set of that Valentino picture, *The Sheik*.

I glimmed the room in search of Irene. Even in such a large expanse, she wasn't hard to spot. Every guy in the joint had his eyes on her. Every woman, too. But for different reasons.

She wore a little black dress so tight the room got ten degrees hotter.

She was talking to some Hollywood big shot. Broad-shouldered. Wavy, grey hair. Studious expression. But this time more friendly. Yeah, I'd seen him before. He was one of the guys Trudy'd pointed out at Harper's party.

Soon as I walked up, Irene immediately stopped talking and kissed me on the cheek. Then she introduced me to the heavy hitter. "Miller, I'd like you to meet a friend of mine. This is William Wade. He directed me in my first picture."

I returned the pleasantries. Gave him my bonafides and shook hands. "Pleasure to meet you, Wade."

We made with the small talk and then Irene had to cut and run. "If you'll excuse me a moment, I have to go powder my nose."

Normally I might've had a beef with her ditching me like that. Especially seeing as how I'd just arrived. But since I wasn't playing the trained monkey this time around, I was willing to make the best of it.

"Certainly, darling," Wade answered. Then he cut his gaze back to me. "I know most of the reporters around here, Miller. You new in town?"

"As a matter of fact, I am. Just moved here a few weeks ago."

"Well then, welcome to Hollywood!" He gave me another firm handshake. "I've lived in this town for thirty years.

Worked my way up from the bottom. Started out as a prop boy back in the silent days."

That's when I suddenly got an idea in my head. Trudy was always trying to get some big shot Hollywood-type to notice her. And here I was tugging mitts with one.

"Listen, I hate to bug a fellow I just met," I told him. "But I've got this friend, a gal who's gonna make a great actress some day. Her name's Trudy Wilkes."

Wade knew exactly what I was getting at. Even if I didn't, I'm sure he'd heard it a thousand times before. "And you'd like for me to give her a screen test."

"Yeah," I nodded, "if that's what you do, sure."

He pondered the idea for a quick minute. Then fished a card out of his inside coat pocket. "I tell you what. Any friend of Irene's is a friend of mine. You tell her to call the Studio and we'll set something up."

I knew Trudy would be over the moon and back again. "Gee, thanks, Mr. Wade! I appreciate this, I really do! If there's anything I can do for you, just let me know."

He chuckled and gave me a good pat on the back. "Well, good press always helps. But who knows? If she works out, you could be doing me a favor! Now if you'll excuse me, my wife is looking very lonely."

"Sure thing, Mr. Wade," I told him. "Thanks again."

After Wade walked off I was left alone nursing my drink. I'll admit, I stuck out like a balloon at a needle convention.

Luckily, Irene was back in no time. And with a certain twinkle in her optics. Like she was ready for a little trouble. "So, how was your conversation with Mr. Wade?" she asked.

"It was great," I told her. "He's a real nice fellow."

She gave me a wicked grin. Steamy. Sultry. Hungry. Then she backed away. "Come on. Let's get out of here."

"Say, where're you going?" I asked.

She stopped and looked back at me. Gave me another look over her perfectly smooth shoulder. Hot enough to melt the Hudson in January. I had to adjust my collar.

"Follow me," she whispered. Low. Breathy.

THE CITY BURNS AT NIGHT

WE LEFT the club, cut through the lobby, turned a few corners. The halls were wide and spacious. Twice the size of what you find in New York. Next thing I know, we're in some dead end corridor. Alone. But who knew for how long?

She pressed me up against the wall. Then backed away to the one opposite. Made sure I had a real good view. Had to wonder what she was up to. I didn't have to wonder long.

"You really disappointed me yesterday," she chastised. "Don't you find me attractive?"

"Yeah, of course, Baby," I told her. "But — "

"But what?" she complained.

"You're a married woman," I reminded her.

"I'm a married woman who gets around," she cooed. "You *remember* that."

"You're making it pretty hard," I told her. And more ways than one.

"Show me," she commanded.

I just stood there like an idiot. Not knowing what to say. Or especially what she was asking me to do. We might've been alone at the moment, but this was still a public establishment. They have laws, you know.

She reached up slowly. Then tugged at one of the straps on her dress. It hung there on that perfect shoulder. Like it just didn't want to let go.

Until it finally did. And dropped down across her bare arm.

I looked down the hall to make sure no one was coming.

They weren't. Not yet, anyways.

Would've hated for someone to stroll up and spoil the moment.

"Don't look away," she begged. "Please." She reached up slowly again. Tugged at the other strap.

It held on longer this time. Until it finally didn't and dropped, too.

Her dress gave way. It fell seductively, just across her shapely womanly charms. One slight move and it would fall right down. All the way to the floor.

This time I didn't look away.

This gal had an adventurous streak a mile wide and then some.

And I was ready to follow wherever she wanted to lead me.

"Come closer," she instructed.

I took a few steps forward and stopped. Just a foot or two away. Almost close enough to touch. But still far enough back.

"Closer than that," she added.

I took a few more steps. This time we were only inches apart.

My lamps were locked on that dress. So precarious. With every breath I thought for sure it would drop.

She looked up at me. Stared deep into my oculars. By this point, I was putty in her soft little mitts.

She reached up. Gently ran her fingers across my chest. Sent chills up my spine and then some.

That's when I finally broke.

I grabbed her luscious figure and pulled her into my arms.

And then I kissed her.

Kissed her like I'd never kissed a woman before.

A WHILE later, we made our way back to the Grove. I dropped her off at the powder room so she could freshen up. Didn't want it to look obvious.

I was first back at the club. Straightened my Windsor and made a beeline for the bar. Definitely needed a quick drink. Could have sworn Wade gave me a nod as I walked by. But maybe he was just being friendly.

A few minutes later I spotted Irene step back in. She mingled her way through the crowd. Threw a quick glance my way and posed for a couple of photos.

I downed the last of my Scotch and worked my way towards the band. Where it was most crowded. Wasn't too long before Irene had shimmied back in my direction.

That's when the band picked up with a catchy tune. Perfect timing. "I feel like dancing," she told me. "You do dance, don't you, Mr. Miller?"

"Yeah, Sure," I told her. I did at that and a whole lot more.

I took her by the slender mitt and led her out to the dance

floor. We'd just done a few steps when I suddenly got an uneasy feeling. Didn't like the looks we were getting.

I tried to shrug it off. With her in my arms it wasn't hard.

We jiggled across the floor a bit longer. Next thing I know, we were back in range of a pair of old geezers. Both of them giving me the stink eye.

At that point I was ready to knock the old man flat. I didn't care how ancient he was. Teach them both a lesson.

I didn't know if Irene saw them, too. But she definitely sensed something had set me on edge. "What's wrong?" she asked.

I nodded towards the relics. "They're glaring at us."

"Don't worry about them," she scoffed. "They just like to stare because they don't have lives of their own anymore."

I steered her away, back to the middle of the dance floor. Just looking into her peepers made me forget the whole business. Those peepers that had made a million guys swoon when they'd watched her up on the big screen. And here she was, right there in my arms.

That's when she leaned in and whispered, "Kiss me."

I looked back at her in surprise. "Here, in front of all these people?"

She just laughed it off. "Of course! Everyone here fools around. Besides, most of them are too drunk to even notice."

I glanced around. This time the geezers were nowhere in sight. Must've been past their bedtime.

Then she said it louder. If nothing else than to make her point. "Kiss me."

Still, I was having a hard time buying it.

Okay, the hallway was one thing. Even if it was a little dangerous. We were there alone. And luckily managed to stay that way. But this was different. Right out in the open. And there were camera boys everywhere.

"I don't know," I stammered.

"Kiss me," she insisted. "Kiss me and I'll be *yours*."

Oh, what the hell? No man in his right mind could resist a dame like that. Not even standing in front of the Pope.

I'd just leaned in to lay one on her when she slapped me hard across the map. "How dare you!" she screamed.

I grabbed her mitt before she could do it again. "What the

hell was that for?"

I'd seen some crazy dames in my day, but this one took the cake. One minute she's undressing in front of me. And the next she's causing bodily injury.

I didn't know *what* to make of it. Was sure there'd still be a hand print in the morning.

Irene jerked her mitt free and stormed out of the club.

This time I didn't have to suspect it. Everyone in the club *was* watching me. And wondered what I'd just done to deserve such a show of force.

The pair of old geezers sure managed to get an eyeful. Especially the old woman. "Serves him right! She's a married woman!"

I'd had enough. I wasn't about to take it anymore. I gave 'em an earful of my own on the way out the door.

"What are you people looking at?"

CHAPTER TWENTY

I DIDN'T know what was up with our *scene* at the party but I wasn't about to stick around and find out. I hightailed it back to my teepee and calmed down with a bottle of bourbon.

Soon as I made it back to my stash, I tossed my wallet and keys on the kitchen counter. Then reached for the nearest bottle. No sooner had I downed my first swig than the horn jingled.

"Miller Mansion," I grumbled. "*Jeeves* speaking."

It was Trudy. Boy was I glad to hear her voice. She was even happier to hear mine. Though it was hard to tell with all the worry and concern.

"Tom, are you okay?" she asked. "I haven't heard from you in two days."

"Yeah, Trudy. I'm fine," I reassured her. "I've just been putting in a lot of hours on this Arson story."

Had to admit, I was really feeling like a louse. Here I am playing peek-a-boo with Irene in the hallway, and poor Trudy's sitting at home worried sick.

We hadn't exactly stood in front of the preacher or anything, but still. I wanted to make it up to her. And I had just the ticket. "Hey, look, I was just getting ready to call you. I got some good news."

"Oh?" she asked. I could hear her voice light up already.

"Yeah, Doll," I explained. "You see, I met this film director to-night, and he says he'd like to give you a screen test."

She practically jumped through the horn on that one. Was sorry I hadn't told her in person. "A screen test? Oh, my heavens! Who was it?"

"His name was Wade, or something like that," I told her. "He said to call his office in the morning."

"You met *William Wade*?" She shouted so loud I thought she was going to wake the neighbors. "And he wants to give me a screen test? Oh, Tom! This is just so wonderful! I don't know what to say!"

"You're on your way up, Sweetheart," I told her. "Top of the world! Let me give you the number. It's HOllywood 4-8687."

She was still beside herself. "Where on earth did you you meet him?"

"Oh, I was at this party at the Grove and —" That's when I realized I'd opened my yap instead of using my brain. Right away I could hear the confusion in her voice. "A party? What kind of party?"

"Nothing much," I told her. "Uh, I was just there working. Trying to follow up on a lead."

Not sure she completely bought it, but she made like she did anyways. "Oh, I see."

"Yeah," I told her, "he gave me his card and said for you to call —"

And that's when I made dumb play #2. I reached for my wallet to nab Wade's card. And knocked the horn over.

I grabbed the receiver off the floor. "Trudy? Trudy? Aww, nuts!" Just my luck, I'd hung up on her. I was about to dial her back when it rang again. "Sorry about that, Trudy," I answered.

"So, that's who you were talking to," she said. Only it wasn't Trudy. It was Irene.

I would've hung up on *her* and called Trudy back. But there was something I just had to ask. "Say, what's the big idea slapping me at the party like that?"

That's when she cued the waterworks again. "Oh Tom, I'm so sorry! But I had to leave quickly and make sure that everyone was watching me. I didn't know what else to do!"

If you thought I turned into a complete sucker the minute

a dame starts bawling, you'd be right. Just put me on a stick and wrap me in cellophane.

"What d'you mean you had to leave quick?" I asked her. "What are you talking about?"

That's when she dropped the bomb on me. Like a ton of bricks. "Kellman was there. He was watching me *dance* with you."

I couldn't believe my lobes. Was this dame pulling another fast one on me? Or was she actually telling the truth? Or did it even matter? "Kellman? You saw him at the party?"

"I'm sorry, Tom," she sobbed. "But I was scared. I just had to get out of there."

There was only so much I could do over the horn. Especially if she was lying. Even more if she was telling the truth. There was just no way around it. I had to see her in person.

"Look, we need to talk," I told her.

I could hear the relief in her voice right away. "You'd do that for me?"

"Sure Doll, anything," I assured her. "Just you name it and I'll hightail it to wherever you are."

"Okay," she sniffled, "but you can't come here."

I'd figured that one already. I glanced around my digs. Wasn't exactly the Taj Mahal, but it wasn't too shabby. Especially if I took a few minutes to straighten up before she darkened my doorstep.

"You could come to my place...." I suggested.

I needn't have worried. She had other ideas. "I know. Why don't we meet somewhere?"

"Yeah, sure," I told her.

Before I could throw out a suggestion, she had one of her own. "I know just the place. It's downtown. It's called the Midnight Motel."

The Midnight Motel.

I still wanted to call Trudy back, but I wasn't about to miss out on the Kellman story. Figured I'd let Ma Bell take the heat for that one. I swigged down the last of my hooch and made for the portal.

I was ready to finally get some answers.

I BOOKED it over to the Motel as fast I could and parked across the street. The place looked pretty quiet. Was sure I must've gotten there first. No sign of Irene.

But then I glimmed a dark figure peeking out from behind the bungalows. A very shapely figure. In a short pink jacket. And a tight black dress.

It was Irene, all right.

Soon as she lamped me, she ran straight over and jumped in my bucket. I could tell right away she was scared. Shivering like a four-year-old at a Frankenstein picture.

"How'd you get here?" I asked. "Where's your car?"

"I took a cab," she sobbed, then jumped straight into my arms. "Oh, Tom! I'm so frightened."

"Frightened of what?" I had to ask.

She took a moment to collect herself. To grab a tissue from her purse and wipe her beautiful optics.

"I'm scared Kellman may find me," she finally explained. "And even more scared of what he might do."

"Don't worry," I reassured her, "nothing's gonna happen. I'll see to that, I promise."

She hugged me even tighter. "I just don't know what to do. I'm afraid to sleep in my *own home*."

I lifted her chin and stared into those peepers that'd made millions of guys want to howl at the moon. "I tell you what. I'll get you a room here at the motel. You can stay here as long as you like. Now don't you worry about a thing."

I got out of my bucket and hoofed it back over to the office. Gabbed a few minutes with my old chubby-necked pal. Then I threw some geetus his way, enough to cover to the end of the week.

MINUTES LATER, I was marching Irene across the threshold of good ole Bungalow 16. Couldn't have worked out better if I'd planned it.

The digs were small and cozy. Better than I expected. Just big enough for one bed with a blue-checkered blanket, a few pictures of ducks on the wall, and a vase of fresh gardenias on the table. Not too shabby by my standards.

But I should've known her standards were a different matter. Even if she was the one who suggested it. "You gonna be okay here by yourself?" I asked.

She turned back to me with a scared look in her baby blues. "I think I'd feel a lot safer if I knew you were going to be here with me."

"Well, I don't know about that," I replied. There were about a million reasons why this wasn't a good idea. Her husband for starters. Not to mention Kellman. Or Trudy.

She gave me a pout that would make a priest give in. "Please?"

What else could I do? I'll admit it. I was putty in her hands. And excited about the possibilities.

"Yeah, all right," I gave in. I was easy. Too easy. "But just for a while. I gotta be at work in the morning. Bright and early."

"Thank you," she gave me a quick peck on the cheek and made herself at home. Took off her jacket and pulled back the covers on the bed. Then she stopped a minute and wrinkled her pretty little nose.

"I don't seem to have anything to sleep in. Could I borrow your shirt for the evening?"

"Uh... yeah, sure," I took off my coat and tie, then unbuttoned my Oxford. Wasn't exactly crazy about heading home in my undershirt, but that was the least of my worries. I tossed it to her.

"Thank you," she took it. "If you'll excuse me a minute?"

"Sure, go right ahead." She popped into the powder room and shut the door.

I wasn't sure why the sudden flush of modesty, but I wasn't going to argue. We were already treading into dangerous territory.

Well, the chair didn't look too comfortable, but I'd slept in worse. I'd just sat down good when she came back out. Wearing my Oxford. And little else.

She crawled onto the bed and gave me the stare down. "What are you doing in that chair?" she cooed. "The bed is much more comfortable."

"I'm not so sure," I countered.

"Please, come over here with me," she purred. "I promise I'll behave."

"Nothing doing, Sweetheart." I just pulled my lid down

over my optics.

She hit me with those peepers again. "Please, Tom. I can't sleep all by myself."

"But you're not alone," I told her. "I'm *right* here."

"But you're *all the way* across the room in the chair. You know it's not comfortable."

She had me there. But I wasn't about to argue.

She sat up and fingered the top button on her buttondown. *My button-down.* "There's plenty of room on the bed."

I did my best to ignore her. But there was only so much more a man could take. She was plenty irresistible up on the movie screen. But in person? Even a eunuch wouldn't stand a chance.

And she knew it, too.

This time she crawled right up to the edge and gave me the stare down. "You'll be much better over here beside me. And I'll be better off, too."

"Oh, all right," I finally gave in. Wasn't going to end any other way.

I walked around and settled in on the other side. Thought about keeping one foot on the floor, but that was just too uncomfortable.

It didn't matter, anyways. Irene rolled right over. Next thing I knew she was nuzzled up close. I could feel every ounce of her womanly charms pressed up tight against me.

"Won't you hold me?" she purred.

"I thought you said you were going to behave?" I asked.

She just tittered softly. "You should know better than to trust me by now."

She was right. I should.

She rolled over some more and kissed me. Softly at first. Then deeper. Wetter. Until she took my breath away.

That's when I finally gave in. I wrapped my arms around her and kissed her long and hard. Just the way a woman who looks like that needs to be kissed. And the way it should be done.

This was it. I knew I might regret it in the morning. Or even just an hour later. But there was no backing down. And I was going to enjoy the hell out of every second of it. She even more so.

After a good several minutes things had really hit the boiling point. Her chemise was halfway off and there were at least three torn buttons on the floor.

That's when she finally had to stop and come up for air. She was breathing so hard I thought she'd need oxygen.

But the smile on her face told me there was no stopping before we'd finished the job.

Then she looked at me with those gorgeous peepers and whispered breathlessly, "Well, I need to get some sleep. Good-night."

Then she gave me another deep kiss and just rolled over. Left me like a big sap just laying there.

High and dry.

CHAPTER TWENTY-ONE

THE NEXT MORNING, I left while Irene was still dozing. Needless to say, I didn't get much sleep. I was more frustrated than a one-armed paper hanger. That was twice she'd played me. And both in the same night.

As much as I wanted to stay there and play house, I still had a story to chase. And an editor who was getting short on patience.

So I ran by my digs for another Oxford and a clean shave. The new one wasn't too fresh, but at least it had all its buttons. And it wasn't wrapped around a beautiful, sleeping dame in a seedy motel.

Also called Trudy with all the particulars on her screen test. And let Ma Bell take the heat for our broken connection.

It didn't matter. She was too excited to be sore. Told her I'd drop by later to check in and get the skinny.

Then it was straight to the office. Had I known I was in for a "warm reception," I would've steered clear of the place.

I'd just gotten out of my crate and was ankling it into the edifice when the missing face of Mt. Rushmore stepped in my path. "You Tom Miller?" he asked. "You work here at the *Chronicle*, don't you?"

I gave him the up and down. He was about my height, larger build. Well dressed, but obviously knew his way around the neighborhood. Map made of granite.

"Yeah, that's me," I told him. "Who's asking?"

"I got a message for you," he barked.

That's when his anvil-for-a-fist sucker punched me square in the gut. I barely had time to react before he decked me again upside the cranium.

I was already seeing stars and swung at whatever I could. It was no use. I was just swimming in cobwebs. He slugged me at least twice more.

Next thing I knew I was tasting blood and concrete. Lying flat on the sidewalk like a 98 pound chump.

"That's from Frank Kellman," he laughed. Then he got back in his jalopy and sped off.

I tried to lamp the plate number, but my cranium had more constellations than the Walk of Fame.

A WHILE later I finally stumbled back into the news room. I'd stopped by the facilities to clean off the blood. But there was no covering up the fact that I'd just had a date with a steamroller.

But at least I knew I was on the right track. Had the shiner to prove it.

Was hoping to go right to my desk and just cool my dogs for bit. With Irene stashed at the motel and Kellman hot on my heels, I needed a minute to figure out my next move.

No such luck.

Jenkins glimmed me just as soon as I darkened the portal. And he was madder than a hornet in a rain storm. "Miller! Where the heck have you been? I tried calling you till all hours of the morning!"

"Sorry, Mr. Jenkins," I told him, rubbing my kisser. "I was covering another angle."

"Yeah, well, I hope it was important," he barked, "because there was another fire last night. An old bungalow down on Mulholland."

That was just great. I'd missed out on the action twice in one night. He should've fired me on the spot.

"I finally had to send Pinkman out to cover it," he grumbled. "And what happened to your face?"

"Some big lunk was waiting for me out front this morning,"

I explained. "With a message from Frank Kellman."

"Maybe I ought to take you off this story," Jenkins groused, shaking his noggin.

That was the last thing I wanted. I didn't just get handed my lunch for nothing. "Look, I'm sorry about missing the scoop, Mr. Jenkins. But please, I know I'm on the right track."

At least there was one good thing about getting dropped like a sack of potatoes. "Last night I found out Kellman's been after Irene Faye," I told him. "Now it's only a matter of time before he shows his face. Then we've got our story."

"I just hope you live to write it," Jenkins sighed. "You've got one more day, Miller. And if you don't have something solid by then, you'll be writing obituaries. Starting with your own!"

Soon as I'd sat back down at my desk, Gronchi sidled up and just shook her cute little noggin. "Girl trouble?" She might've been ribbing, but she wasn't that far off the mark.

"Any luck with that George Matthews fellow?" I asked. "The one who was checked into that shady motel?"

For a second I thought I was going to get another shiner.

"Yeah, I know the one," she smirked. "I ran all the plates. No George Matthews, no Frank Kellman, or anything else. Just a broom salesman, a pickle maker, and three different lugs cheating on their wives."

Well, there you had it. If Gronchi couldn't dig it up, there was nothing to be found.

That didn't matter, though. I was sure Kellman was our man. I was willing to bet money on it.

I just had to figure some way to get him to show his mug.

Then she slapped a pile of messages on my desk. "Plus, that detective keeps calling for you. I'm not your secretary, you know."

She was, actually. But I wasn't about to argue the point.

I'd already had my keister handed to me once that morning. I wasn't about to sign up for an encore.

CHAPTER TWENTY-TWO

AFTER I'd spent enough in-person coinage, I was finally able to skip out and make tracks. I wanted to head back to the motel and check on Irene. But after the horn shenanigans, I owed it to Trudy to drop in on her first. Luckily, she was still working the lunch shift at Schwab's.

It was my first time in the place. This was the original locale on Sunset and Crescent. The Schwab brothers built a few more around town, but the Hollywood types and the starving hopefuls all frequented the original digs. Fellow newshound Sidney Skolsky warmed a stool here for his column in *Photoplay*. My kind of guy.

The joint was long and narrow, with the pharmacy on one side and the more popular lunch counter on the other. The place was packed with young kids fresh off the bus and then some. All with the same starry-eyed look in their optics, giving me a desperate once-over when I ankled in through the portal. All on the chance I might be somebody in the business.

Trudy was just dishing up a cup of joe at the counter as I squeezed my way through the crowd. I hijacked a stool and tipped back my lid. That's when she got a load of my shiner. Practically dropped the coffee pot. "Oh, Tom! What happened?"

"Oh, some big lugs jumped me going in to work this morning," I explained. "Want me to back off the story I'm working on. It's nothing."

She called over to the cute little red-haired number working next to her. "Sheila, you mind watching the counter for a minute?"

Sheila nodded her approval. Then Trudy proceeded to play nurse and shoved me towards an empty booth in the corner.

"You look awful," she commented. "Are you sure you're all right?"

"Yeah, I'm fine," I assured her. "Look, I'm sorry again about last night. I don't know what happened. I tried to call you back, but I couldn't get through."

Truth of the matter was, I felt really bad about ditching out on her like that. I didn't like fibbing like I did, but I sure couldn't tell her the truth.

"It's okay," she replied. "You never know with the phone lines these days."

"I could use a good hot cup of java, though, and maybe a sandwich."

"Sure, I'll get it for you right away," she told me. The mother hen inside her was already out in full force. She'd barely gotten two steps before she pirouetted on her pretty little heels and plopped right back down in front of me.

"Oh, I almost forgot!" she exclaimed. "I called William Wade, the director, and guess what? He wants to give me a screen test! This evening at 5:30!"

"Say Doll, that's first-rate!" I told her.

"Yes, and I owe it all to you!" she chirped. "Now, you just sit right there. I'll have your coffee and sandwich in a jiffy."

That Wade had really come through. Just like he promised. I sure owed him one.

Of course, it never entered my grey matter that he might have ulterior motives. Should have, but didn't.

But he'd get what was coming to him anyways.

SOON as I stepped outside the joint, I was ready to make tracks back to the motel to check on Irene. Only I didn't get far. Thanks to a familiar looking tan coupe squatting right next to my jalopy. I didn't have to think twice about who held the pink slip.

Long legs and midnight tresses. The view only got better the further up you went.

"Girlfriend give you a steak sandwich for that shiner?" Flora Mason asked.

My first thought was to just ignore her. But I should've known that idea was a one-way ticket to nowhere. Besides, there was no ignoring a doll like that. And she knew it.

"Good thing, huh?" she prodded. "Harder to notice the paw print on your puss."

"What're you getting at, Doll?" I snapped.

I figured if she'd really wanted to make trouble, she'd have staged this little ambush inside. Center stage, with Trudy in the front row. Orchestra seat.

Instead, she was just trying to shake me up. Had to give this dish credit. She was doing a pretty good job of it, too.

She wasn't the first dame reporter I'd run across in my day. But darn if she didn't put her fair share of hombres to shame.

What bothered me was just how much she knew. Or thought she knew, at least. But that turned out to be very little.

"Got to hand it to you, Shamus," she smiled as she sidled up towards me. "I was a little worried when you got in to talk to the Mrs. But judging by the bruises on that map of yours, I'd say you struck out worse than I did."

CHAPTER TWENTY-THREE

WHEN I finally made it back to the motel, the place was quiet as a church on Halloween. Not a single bucket in the lot.

I didn't know what I was doing back there. Sometimes I think I must be a glutton for punishment. Still, I had to make sure she was all right.

I went back to Bungalow 16 and dusted the portal. There wasn't any answer, so I rapped again. This time a little louder.

"Irene, it's me."

All of a sudden the portal swung open and I found myself staring face-to-face with a giant wall of flesh. The guy was dressed only in his skivvies and fuming mad.

"I don't know who you are," he grunted, "but there ain't no Irene here."

Then I heard a high, chirpy voice call out from behind him. "Pookie-Bear, who's at the door?"

He glowered down at me and clenched his stone-like fists. "No one, darling. Just some bum."

I couldn't back away fast enough. "Geez, sorry, Big Fella. My apologies, really."

I'd just gotten clear of his reach when a question got the better of me. I just had to toss it out there before he slammed the hatch.

"Say, you're not George Matthews, are you?" I asked.

The size of his enormous dukes and the scowl on his mug told me it wouldn't pay to wait for an answer. I backed away quickly and high-tailed it back to my crate.

I lit up a gasper and ran the current circumstances through my grey matter. Figured Irene must not have been too scared, because she sure didn't stick around long. What bothered me more was I'd paid for the week. Was sure there was no getting that lettuce back in my garden.

But where'd she lam off to? Her place? Some other dive in another part of town? And why powder on me in the first place?

AS LONG as I was there, I decided to see if my old pal at the front desk knew anything. No doubt another sawbuck or two would get me some answers. I just hoped it was something useful.

"Excuse me," I inquired, "but I rented Bungalow 16 last night for a young lady friend, and she's not there anymore."

"Right, Mr. Miller," he chimed. He remembered me well. And I should hope so. He'd already cost me plenty without much in return.

"Any idea when she dusted?" I queried.

"Let's see," he replied. "Just let me check the registry."

He flipped it open and ran his chubby finger down the page. "Bungalow 16. Yes, she checked out earlier this morning. She left you a message."

"Oh, yeah?" I tipped my lid back in surprise. Was sure she was playing me for a chump again.

He reached into the mail slots behind him, pulled out a folded piece of white paper. Handed it to me, with a little flourish to boot. "Here you are."

I thanked him as I took it. It was a handwritten note. On her personal stationery.

Meet me at my place to-night, 7:00pm sharp. Irene.

CHAPTER TWENTY-FOUR

I TOLD Trudy I'd take her to the Studio for her screen test. There was no way she could've finished her shift and made it on time taking the Red Car. Not without grabbing a hack.

I worried for a second about keeping my own date with destiny. But it was all jake. I had plenty of time to drop Trudy off and still make it over to Irene's.

I hoisted her into my chariot right on the five o'clock dinner bell. We made tracks down Fairfax, then didn't spare the horsepower all the way down Melrose. Pulled up right outside the Metropolitan gates at twenty after. Right on time and in clear view of the Hollywoodland Sign.

"You nervous?" I asked her.

"Of course, I'm nervous," she chided me. "What do you think, Silly?"

"Don't you worry about a thing, Sweetheart," I assured her. "Just go in there and knock 'em dead. You'll do great, I know it."

She gave me a sweet smile. "Thanks, Tom."

"Say, you need a ride home?" I asked. I wasn't sure how that would work with Irene. But I couldn't just leave her sitting there high and dry.

"No, that's okay," she assured me. "I'll just take the Red Car. Or get a cab."

"Who knows," I smiled, "you might even go home in a limo to-night."

"Wouldn't that be something?" she laughed. "Whatever happens, I know I owe it all to you. Thank you!"

That's when she leaned over and planted one hell of a smooch right on my kisser.

I was still enjoying the after-effects when she suddenly got a panicked look on her puss. No idea what could have spooked her all of a sudden. "What's the worry, Doll?"

"Oh, I bet I smudged my lipstick," she worried. "I better check it before I go in there."

I reached for the visor. "You need a mirror, Baby?"

"No thanks," she replied and fished into her purse. She pulled out her tiny compact and surveyed the damage.

Looked fine to me, but her assessment was another story. "Oh, my heavens, I don't want to go in looking like this!"

She pulled out her lipstick and went to work like Da Vinci. Of course, it helped to have such a flawless canvas. She puckered up a few times to check her handiwork. Once she'd given it the a-okay, she dug into her purse again.

This time, she came up empty-handed.

"Oh, I don't have a tissue," she panicked. "Do you have some paper? Just anything I can use to soften my lipstick?"

Now it was my turn. I didn't want this little doll going in anywhere near less than perfect. I quickly searched my jalopy and came up short. I didn't even have a snot rag on me.

Then I dug into my pockets. Only thing I had was a folded scrap of paper.

"Uh, sure," I said and handed it to her. "Here."

She pressed her beautiful lips down on the paper and left two perfect little red imprints. "There, that's better. Thanks!"

"Good luck! I told her. "I'll call you later, and then we can go out and celebrate!"

"You've got a deal!" she answered as she opened the door and got out. She leaned back in the window and blew me a kiss. "I love you!"

And then she was off. A hurried angel that left only the smell of her perfume in her wake.

But what hung even heavier was her sudden profession of ardor as she'd left my presence.

I don't know if she'd even realized she'd said it.

But either way, one thing was clear. This doll had actually fallen for me.

Overhead, the skies were getting cloudy and dark. There was a storm brewing. It doesn't rain that often in L.A. Should have realized then it was a bad omen.

Should have. But didn't.

I GOT to the Saltzman mansion right on time. Seven o'clock sharp. Sun was just going down. The place looked quieter than a monastery in the dead of winter. The evening skies were getting darker and the muffled sound of thunder echoed off in the distance.

Was surprised to find the front door ajar. Figured that was my invite to come on in. I figured right.

The lights were out in the foyer and everything was dark. I kept telling myself I was just there for a story. Yeah, right.

Thankfully, there was no sign of Old Derek. No sign of the butler, either. The place still looked empty, but I knew better.

Something was definitely up. I just wasn't sure what.

I'd just made it into the foyer when Irene called down from upstairs. "Right on time. I like that in a man."

I looked up the circular stairwell. Nothing but shadows. I still couldn't see her. Could only hear her voice. Giggling. Taunting.

Just then something came plunking down the steps. It landed on a rung near the bottom.

It was one of her heels. Sleek and red.

"Oh, I dropped my shoe," she cooed. "If I'm not careful, I might drop something else."

Clearly, that was my invitation to follow. "Don't worry, I'll be sure to catch it," I called up.

I heard her laugh and run away down the hall. What else was I going to do? I had to investigate.

I'd gotten halfway up the stairs when I found something else. One of her black silk stockings.

When I reached the top landing, there was still no sign of her. Just another stocking.

She'd left me a trail of clothing. All I had to do was follow.

THE CITY BURNS AT NIGHT

Clearly this gal liked to play games. And I was all too willing to roll the dice along with her.

"Irene?" I called out. No telling where she was hiding.

That's when I noticed something red on the floor. Something linen.

Her skirt.

A few more steps took me to her blouse. White and silky.

Next was her black lace brassiere.

I finally reached the bedroom at the end of the hall. The portal was slightly ajar.

A pair of obsidian silk skivvies hung on the knob. Told me I was in the right place.

I pushed the portal open and stepped inside. "Irene?"

The room was mostly dark. Just a small shaft of fading sunlight came in through the giant picture window. Hard to make out the details. But I could grasp the big picture.

From what I could tell, this was one of the swankiest digs in the whole mansion. Straight across from me was a huge four poster bed. Complete with silk canopy. Kind you'd expect in the boudoir of Marie Antoinette.

To my left was a walk-in closet and private powder room. Followed by a tall, ornate dresser and wide vanity. Across the room was a couch and a chair. Plus a fireplace with a little gold man standing proudly on the mantle.

All told, it was easily bigger than my apartment stash.

I could just make out her figure hidden in shadows. Lying on the bed. Curled up under the satin sheets.

She sat up when I came in. Waiting and ready.

"I thought you'd never get here."

CHAPTER TWENTY-FIVE

IRENE eased off the bed like a siren dipping into the ocean. She took the sheet with her. Never took her glims off me. Not for a second.

When she touched the floor, she did a graceful little pirouette. Like a seductive ballet. As she twirled around, the smooth bed linen wrapped itself around her luscious frame.

I didn't know what could be softer. The warm silk or her bare skin.

Then she stepped over in front of the window. Into the fading light where I could see her better. Gave me a lot to consider. And how.

One thing was for sure. She knew how to make one hell of an entrance.

"I thought you were afraid to come back here," I queried.

"I knew I'd be safe with you," she purred. "Besides, I wanted to make love to you in my own bed. And not in some strange motel room."

She also knew how to get to the point.

I loosened my tie, threw my lid on the dresser. But soon as I ankled a step closer, she backed further away, yodeled her displeasure. "Not so fast. I want to savor every moment."

She twirled again. Slowly. Let the sheet swirl around her. And the moonlight dance quietly across the alabaster skin of her bare back.

Then she took the ends of the sheet and twirled slowly once more. This time she let it unravel, but was careful enough to keep it under her dainty chin.

Finally, she held it all the way up like a curtain. Her gorgeous, naked form perfectly outlined in silhouette. Like shadows on a movie screen. Only better. And right in front of me.

But that was nothing compared to the way she moved behind it. Every delicious curve swaying gracefully for my pleasure. "See anything you like?" she tempted.

Nothing could've wiped the stupid grin off my map. "Oh, yeah."

"Would you like to see more?"

"Absolutely," I told her.

She laughed playfully and dropped the sheet to her shoulders. Then she raised it back up under her chin.

I instinctively moved forward, but she quickly took another step back. "No no, not until I say so."

I was putty in her dainty little claws.

She pulled the sheet up tight to her neck and spun around again. This time she gave me a full view of her shapely backside.

It was all I could do to contain myself.

"So," she teased, "you want to see more?"

"Yeah, of course," I confirmed.

She let the whole thing drop down to her navel. Gave me a good long look at her womanly charms before she pulled it back up to her neck again.

"Saw a lot that time, didn't you?" she giggled.

I'll admit it, I was too entranced to pay attention to anything else. Like the sound of a jalopy outside. Or the front portal swinging open.

Just when I thought she'd teased me enough, she let it fall to her navel the second time. That's when I couldn't take it anymore. I charged straight for her.

I sailed across the room and took her tight in my arms. The sheet just fell to the floor.

She was helpless in my grasp. I scooped her right up. Carried her back to the bed.

I laid her back down, strong but gentle. I stared into those beautiful peepers once more. Then I kissed her.

Long and passionate. The kind of kiss that makes you forget everything else.

Almost.

But the longer I kissed her, and caressed the soft skin of her luscious curves, the more I was entranced by her unbelievable beauty.

Millions of guys had watched her on the big screen and could only dream of a night like this. And here I was, with her in the flesh. Naked in my arms. All mine for the taking.

I was just about to go in for the score when a little thought suddenly took hold. And scratched hard at the back of my noggin. And wouldn't let go.

Only it wasn't Trudy. But it should have been. No, this was something else. Danger.

"Wait a minute, what about Kellman?" I had to ask. "Aren't you afraid of what he'll do if he finds us? And what about your husband?"

She nuzzled herself tighter into my grasp. Pulling me back into her spell. Impossible to resist.

"Yes, I am afraid of all that," she told me. "But I can't let it hold me back. I can't let it hold *us* back."

She ran her nimble fingers across the stubble of my chin. Then she kissed me again. And again.

"Please, Tom, you have to understand," she explained. "After I found out that Derek was cheating on me, I thought I could never love again. But thanks to you, I realize that I can!"

I should've expected what she said next. But somehow, I never saw it coming.

"I love you, Tom!" she confessed. "I love *you*!"

I had to take a step back on that one. Trudy had just told me the same thing just a short time earlier. And that one hadn't given me as much pause.

I struggled for the right words. Or just any words, really. "Irene, I don't know what to say…"

I wondered for a moment if she was just playing me again. She was an actress after all. And from what I'd heard, a damn good one. Even had the gold statue to prove it.

But the look in her eyes told me this dame was serious. *Dead serious.*

"Say you love me, too! Please, Tom, just say it!"

"Irene, I..." I struggled for the words.

But then something else hit me. It wasn't a thought or a feeling this time. No, it was something else. And not just the thunder rumbling outside.

"Do you smell kerosene?" I queried.

I'd just gotten up to investigate when the bedroom portal burst wide open. Practically flew off the hinges.

Saltzman!

I LOOKED up to see him standing there. Silhouetted in the hallway light. Angry as fire. A kerosene can in one mitt and a roscoe in the other.

That explained the smell. And a whole lot more.

I tried to form some explanation in my head. But when you're caught in bed with a naked woman, there just isn't much you can say. No talking your way out of it.

I grabbed the sheet off the floor and covered her up.

Saltzman doused the carpet around the bedroom portal but good and ditched the can. I stepped in front of Irene. Worried he might start hosing slugs at any second. Fill both of us full of daylight.

Or worse, light a match.

"What are you doing with my wife?" Saltzman demanded. "Take your hands off her!"

"Derek!" Irene wailed. "What are you doing here?"

"I said take your hands off my wife!" he barked again. He waved the gat for me to move away.

I grabbed for some air and took a step forward. Put some distance between the two of us. But still not leave her defenseless.

And hopefully figure a way out of this catastrophe.

I was just glad it wasn't Kellman.

Was sure I could take Saltzman. I had him by a good foot. And he was about as tough as a paper dandelion. But I needed to get closer. And he looked awful nervous on that trigger. Didn't want him to get wiggy and start squirting iron.

"Try to keep him talking," I whispered.

He waved us towards the window. "All right, both of you, get over there! And for heaven's sake, put something on! You horrid little trollop!"

Again, not exactly the kind of chin music you'd expect from a guy born in Brooklyn. Even if he was second generation. But I had too much else toiling my grey matter to give it much thought.

Saltzman grabbed her skivvies off the doorknob and a red dress from the open walk-in. Tossed them both on the bed. I kept my ground in front of Irene, just for the sake of modesty. Even if he was her spouse.

By the time she'd gotten presentable, Irene was already in tears. "What are you doing here, Derek?" she sobbed.

"I came back to torch this place," he growled. "What's it look like I'm doing?"

I thought I'd had this thing figured out. But this little twist really took me by surprise. "You?" I asked. "You've been setting all these fires? But why?"

"For the insurance money, why else?" he confessed. "I've got some heavy gambling debts I've got to pay off."

Couldn't believe he was so forthcoming. Like he wanted to get it all on the record.

I didn't even have to beat it out of him.

Then he jabbed the heater in my direction again. "You may not know this, but I own a piece of every building that went up. Only the cops think it was Kellman. Out to get *me* so he can get to my wife!"

I couldn't believe my lobes. "But that apartment! There were kids in there! They were almost killed!"

"Kids with deadbeat parents who don't pay their rent!"! he snarled. "Take your sob story to someone who cares."

By that point, Irene was practically in hysterics. "Derek, what are you going to do with us?"

Saltzman threw a wicked laugh in our direction. "I figure a couple of bullets will do the trick. By the time the cops find what's left of you, no one will be the wiser."

She grabbed onto me tighter than a vice on hot metal. "Oh, Tom! I'm frightened! You can't let him kill us!"

Saltzman screeched again: "I told you once, take your hands off my wife!"

Irene dropped to her knees, bawling. "Please don't hurt us! I'm so sorry, Derek! Please!"

Saltzman just shook his head and sneered. Ready to plug us both right then and there.

He raised up the gat. Got us both in his sights. Finger on the trigger.

And that's when Trudy barged in.

"Tom!" she cried out. "*How could you?*"

CHAPTER TWENTY-SIX

WHAT lousy timing!

Trudy was the last person who needed to get mixed up in all this. In a night full of surprises, this one really took the cake. Or so I thought.

Her sleeve was torn. And mascara ran down her face. From where she'd been bawling the whole way there.

At first I thought it was because she'd caught me there with Irene. Later I found out it was something else entirely.

But first I had to ask: *What the hell was she doing there? And why?*

Irene asked the same question. "Trudy? What's she doing here?"

Talk about a Chinese angle. This situation was getting more hinky by the minute.

"Oh, Tom!" Trudy cried out. "I was afraid I'd find you here. But I just couldn't believe it. Not until I saw it with my own eyes!"

She threw a crumpled note on the floor. I went to pick it up, but Saltzman beat me to it.

"What's this?" he asked.

On one side was a smear of Trudy's lipstick. From where she'd freshened up in the car. On the other side was the note from Irene. Telling me to meet her there at seven.

Like an idiot I'd given it to Trudy.

Of all the rotten luck!

Only it was about to get worse. Thunder rumbled outside. This time louder. And right on cue.

Saltzman looked flustered. He hadn't counted on this little wrinkle. Of course, none of us had.

"You!" he stammered to Trudy. "Get over there! Now! With the other two!"

Trudy looked at him with surprise. This wasn't quite what she'd expected. "Wait, what's going on here?" she asked.

"I'm afraid you came at a bad time, Trudy," I informed her. Of all times for her to get jealous.

Saltzman waved his heater in her direction again. "You heard me. Get over there!

Trudy did as she was told. Then Saltzman pulled a lighter out of his coat pocket. Just what I'd feared. And a whole lot worse.

He was ready to send that whole place up in yet another inferno. And this time with the three of us inside.

Maybe I could understand me and Irene. He'd just walked in on us *in flagrante*. There was no way around that.

But not Trudy. She was perfectly innocent. Wrong place at the wrong time.

I had to get him talking. Every second I could keep Saltzman yammering was another second I could still figure a way to unravel this turmoil.

"Say, didn't your Mom ever teach you not to play with fire?" I asked.

Saltzman fanned the gat back and forth between the three of us. "Okay, which one of you wants it first? How about you, Flyboy?"

"Derek, please!" Irene sobbed again.

"Listen, Saltzman, this is crazy!" I shouted. "I mean, arson is one thing. But this is *murder*!"

That's when Trudy gave me another puzzled look.

"*Saltzman*? That's not Derek Saltzman."

CHAPTER TWENTY-SEVEN

WHAT THE BLAZES? All of a sudden there was yet another twist I hadn't counted on. This whole shebang just wasn't making any sense at all.

"Of course, it is," Irene countered. "I think I *know* my own husband."

"No," Trudy asserted. "I'll admit he looks a lot like him, but that is *not* Derek Saltzman."

And that was it. That one really took the cake. Just when I thought this thing couldn't get any more hinky. It just did.

Maybe Trudy had shown up at the best time after all.

It was high time I got to the bottom of it. "Wait a minute," I queried. "What's going on here?"

"Trust me, Tom!" Irene demanded. "He *is* Derek Saltzman! What does she know? She's just a nobody!"

"I don't know, either." I just shook my head in confusion, finally ready to make my move. "You tell me!"

That's when I charged the fake Saltzman.

"Get away from me — !" he shouted and took a few shots. But all I heard were a bunch of empty clicks.

I decked him hard right across the kisser. Knocked him flat with a solid left hook. He crumpled like a tin can on a railroad track.

I picked up the gat and checked the chamber. Just like I thought. Wasn't even loaded. Thank God.

THE CITY BURNS AT NIGHT 123

Thunder rumbled outside again. Raindrops tapped in rhythm against the window panes.

I still had no idea what was really going on. But I knew enough to realize we were all being played.

And played *but good*.

"This whole thing is an act," I announced. "And that confession from your fake Saltzman here was the grand finale. Okay, Irene. You mind spilling out the truth for a change?"

"All right," she huffed, "now that everything's been *ruined*. She's right. He's not my husband! He's just some two-bit drunk I hired to pretend he was Derek."

That's when it all finally came together. Her whole demeanor turned on a dime. Pleading hysterics one minute. Smirking frustration the next.

"So, you mean to tell me that *you're* the one who's been setting those fires?" I asked.

Irene was dead silent. But the angry look on her beautiful map told me I'd finally hit pay dirt.

"That's right," she confirmed. "I did it to frame Derek. I've been wanting to get back at him ever since he ruined my career. And our marriage."

"So that's what this is about," I realized. "Revenge. Plain and simple."

"Damn right it is," she added. "I figured thirty years or so for arson and insurance fraud is just what he deserved."

"Yeah," I commented. For the first time, it was all *finally* starting to make sense.

Irene continued, "But I knew that putting Derek in the slammer wouldn't be enough, I needed someone on my side. Someone to tell my story. To help put me back on top."

"And that's where I came in," I realized.

"Exactly," she confirmed as she sauntered towards me. "You were perfect. You're new in town. Didn't know the real Derek. You're the perfect witness. Plus, you like to jump into trouble. Reeling you in was the *easiest* part of the plan."

Then she threw her steely gaze back at Trudy. "The only thing I didn't count on was your little *sweetheart* here."

"And what your Fake Saltzman here said about Kellman

— is that true?"

"Most of it," she replied. "The truth is, I did have an affair with the real Kellman. That's how I knew he'd left the country as soon as he got out of prison. He didn't mind me borrowing his name for a while, so long as Derek got his."

That cleared up just about everything. Almost. "And what about George Matthews, the guy you were with at the motel?"

She smiled at me proudly. "Oh, very *good*. You found one of my little red herrings."

Yeah, just like I thought. "Well, it looks like you're going to get your wish after all, Irene. I'm willing to bet your trial makes all the papers."

I was all set to send Trudy down the hallway to ring up Hap Underwood. There was only one thing I hadn't counted on.

Irene still had one more trick up her sleeve. Which is why *she'd* spilled so easily.

"Oh, I don't think so."

She just shook her beautiful noggin and smiled. Don't know when I've ever seen a grin so evil. Then or after.

That's when she reached out to her nightstand and picked up a small, silver lighter.

"Don't forget, this whole house is drenched with kerosene," she reminded us. "Instead of trying to catch me, you need to worry about getting out alive!"

I dove headlong in her direction. Hoped like hell I could stop her. "Irene! No!"

Curse my hulking frame! I was too slow!

She struck the flint. Tossed the flickering torch towards the pool of kerosene by the bedroom portal.

Right beside Trudy.

The whole room went up like a box of matches on the Fourth of July.

CHAPTER TWENTY-EIGHT

I QUICKLY turned heel and grabbed Trudy! Pulled her away from the growing inferno. "Trudy, are you all right?"

She checked her skirt. "I — I think so!" A little singed, but otherwise unharmed.

I grabbed the hacking Fake Salesman by the tunic and yanked him into the clear.

Irene took the opportunity to bolt for the powder room. Slammed the portal shut tight right behind her.

The roaring flames blocked our escape the way we'd come in.

Irene had nabbed the only other way out. I grabbed for the knob, but it wouldn't budge.

Locked!

Damn that Irene! She'd trapped us in there to burn alive!

Smoke choked the room like the honeymoon suite at San Quentin. Flames latched onto the walls and made quick work of the furniture. It was getting hotter in there by the minute!

If we didn't find another avenue soon, we were goners for sure!

Trudy coughed and cried out, "Oh, Tom! Can you get us out of here?"

I slammed the full heft of my frame against the powder room door. Over and over like a human battering ram. But it was no use. That outlet was locked tighter than Fort Knox!

There was only one other escape route. And it was two stories down.

By this time, the curtains had just caught fire. I jerked them down and threw them into the fireplace. No point in helping the blaze along.

It was gushing outside. Rain pouring down. But not enough to temper the growing blaze inside.

I pulled the sheets off the floor and covered Trudy. I was less concerned about the Fake Saltzman. He just cowered by the bed.

"Stand back, both of you!" I shouted.

I tossed the lamp aside and grappled the night stand. Gave it a good thrust and smashed it right through the windows.

Glass shattered across the room! One shard nearly hit me in the optics! But I was okay.

The rush of air made the flames kick in even higher. We didn't have long to get out of there before we were all yesterday's burnt toast.

I climbed out on the window sill. Tried to get my footing on a small patch of roof. The tiles were so slick I nearly took a dive. Luckily, I managed to catch myself before I went hurtling right over.

"Okay, Trudy, give me your hand!"

I reached out for her dainty wing. But I got Fake Saltzman's instead. He'd shoved his way past her to get out. Stinking coward!

"Mitts off, Bub! Ladies first!" I gave *Ismay* a well-deserved shove. But it was no use. He'd put a death grip on the window sill and wasn't backing off.

"Okay, that's the way you want it!" I told him.

I grabbed him by the collar. Flung him headlong into the hedge-work below. It was enough to break his fall. But not much else.

He climbed out of the foliage and stumbled off. "Thanks, Pal!"

I tell you, I ever run into that coward again, he won't limp away the next time.

THE CITY BURNS AT NIGHT

The flames were getting closer. If it weren't for the rain coming in the window, I don't think we'd have made it.

I reached back for Trudy. Made darn sure I had her good this time. "Come on, I'll lower you down!"

She took one terrified gander and shook her dainty noggin. "Oh, Tom! I can't!"

"You can make it, I promise!"

She waggled her brunette locks again. "I'm too frightened!"

"Listen," I assured her. "I'm not going to let go. Last thing I want to do is leave you up here. I'll lower you down."

This time she shook her beautiful noggin in the affirmative. But the certitude in her glims said so much more.

I don't know why, especially after what she'd just piped, but she *trusted* me. God knows I didn't deserve it.

She reached out and took my paw.

That's when my groundwork gave way. I grabbed for whatever I could. But it was no use. I slid down the roof and crashed cranium first into the foliage below.

I SCRAMBLED out of the bushes. A little worse for wear, but I'd made it.

I lamped upwards to the window. Thank God, Trudy was still there. But at the this point, the blaze was so bright she was just an outline.

"Oh, Tom! Are you okay?" she trembled. I don't know what scared her more. Watching me tumble keister over teakettle. Or knowing what was behind her.

"Yeah, I'm fine!" I called back. But that was the least of my concerns.

Wish like hell I'd just pulled her with me and broken her fall. I'd have preferred a cracked rib or broken collarbone than leaving her up in that window.

I scrambled for a way back up. But everywhere I piped I came up with bupkis. No drain pipe. No latticework. No window ledge. Nothing.

I could run to the garage and search for a ladder. But time was fast running out.

We were down to only one option.

"Okay," I shouted with my arms outstretched. "You've

got to jump! I'll catch you!"

She clutched onto the windowsill. The rain splashed against her beautiful map. The hungry flames right behind her!

"I can't!" she bawled. "It's too high!"

I quickly searched around again. There was just no other option. "Listen to me, Baby! This is the only way! If you don't jump now, you're not going to make it. You hear me?"

She looked back at the encroaching inferno. Her only response was another nod in the affirmative.

Cautiously, she climbed up on the sill. Put one dainty stem out on the wet ledge. The rain was still coming down. Her foot slipped right away.

And then she froze.

"Come on, Baby! You've got to jump!" I bellowed!

She'd grabbed the window frame. Only she wasn't about to let go. Much too terrified to move.

The blaze roared behind her.

Then, in the blink of an eye. She was gone.

Swallowed whole by a giant gust of wretched, black smoke.

Nothing left but the sound of her screams.

CHAPTER TWENTY-NINE

JUST WHEN I thought she was a goner, Trudy burst through that billowing snarl of black smog! She plummeted straight down towards me. Like an angel escaping the fiery infernos of Hell itself. And descended from the thundering clouds above.

She jumped! She'd put all her faith in me and jumped!

She dropped right into my arms. I just stood there for the longest moment. Held her tight as I could. She was safe. Thank God she was safe!

Clutching her just then, I couldn't put her down. Not even with the rain beating down on us. I knew in that moment I just had to come clean.

"Listen, Trudy," I leveled. "You've got to believe me. The only reason I came here to-night was to follow a story. Nothing else. I swear it."

"It's okay, Tom," she replied. "I do believe you. I probably wouldn't if I'd left right away. But after hearing her confess and then trying to kill us, there's no way I *couldn't* believe you."

"You've got to believe me when I tell you something else, too," I added.

"What's that?" she asked.

"You're the only girl for me," I avowed. "I've never had an easy time saying this, but the truth is... I'm falling hard for you, Trudy."

"Oh, I love you, too, Tom!" she exclaimed.

Then she really laid one on me. So hard my knees buckled.

JUST AS I set Trudy back down, Irene sped out of the garage in her tan jalopy. Practically ran us over as she hauled keister out of the driveway.

"Look," I shouted, "we've got to catch Irene! Or I lose the best part of my story!"

I grabbed Trudy by her dainty little mitt. Hauled bunions for my crate. In seconds, I was behind the wheel and we hightailed it after her.

Thanks to the downpour, my windshield was foggier than a September morning in Frisco Bay. Rubbed it down best I could with my coat sleeve. Luckily, I just managed to catch a glimpse of Irene's bucket up ahead as she turned onto Benedict Canyon.

That's when a thought hit me. I'd remembered hearing another jalopy pull up. But there'd been only one other crate in the driveway. Mine.

"Say, how'd you get here anyways?" I asked Trudy.

"I took a cab," she explained. "I told him to wait, but I guess he took off when he saw the house burst into flames." That's when her gorgeous map went wide-eyed as the moon. "Probably thinks I did it."

"Say, how'd it go with your screen test?" I had to ask. "Any word?"

"It was fine," she replied and straightened out her wet skirt. "We'll see."

She wasn't exactly forthcoming with any particulars. I quickly got the gist that it didn't go all that jake. Especially considering her distressed state when she'd arrived.

"Well, did he say anything?" I inquired further. "Give you any hints?"

"Actually," she finally spilled after a long hesitation, "he said it was one of the best he'd ever seen. But I'm sure he was just saying that."

She smoothed out her skirt some more. It was just like the napkin at the Tick Tock all over again.

"What makes you think that?"

"Oh, nothing," she replied, and gave her skirt another

work over. I knew if I pushed too much more, it'd be perma pressed before we ever caught up with Irene.

"What happened to your sleeve?" I queried.

Just as I expected, she brushed me off on that one, too. "Oh, that was nothing. Just snagged it when I was leaving."

I quickly clued in there was a lot she wasn't divulging. I wasn't the only one who'd skimped on a few details. Found out later, that was an understatement. And a whole other story.

Unlike the Cagney picture, this time it wouldn't do any good to keep pressing for answers. She'd come clean when she was ready.

But what I didn't realize at the time was, then it would be too late.

DESPITE the fact that it was darn near impossible to see anything ahead, I kept feeding my bucket a solid stream of ethyl. Rain was pelting down by the bucketful and then some. Made the roads slick as a truckload of rotten banana peels on an August afternoon.

Driving that mountain thoroughfare is no picnic as it is on a sunny day. Even worse in a downpour.

But somehow I managed to keep Irene in my sights. And keep all four wheels on the pavement. Just barely.

Irene turned off onto Mulholland heading towards Hollywood. For those who don't know, Mulholland is a narrow, twisting road that runs for some twenty miles across the top of the Santa Monica Mountains.

It's got the best views of the city on both sides for anyone who wants to stop and take a gander. But it's also notorious for its collection of sharp, twisting curves. And the number of jalopies that end up its many ravines.

Thought for sure Irene would be one of them that night. And if we weren't careful, so would we.

Had no idea where she was going. And after trying to keep up with her on all those hairpin turns, I don't think she did either. She just wanted to get away.

After I fishtailed it more than once, Trudy only got more frightened. I couldn't blame her. "Tom, shouldn't we have called the police?"

"They'd have never caught up with her in time," I informed her. "Besides, the way we're driving, we'll have the cops on our tail in no time."

I could only hope that was actually true.

As we sped through one sharp switchback after another, it was a wonder neither one of us went flying over the mountainside. Just another casualty of Dead Man's Curve.

Mile after mile, twisting turn after twisting turn, I kept her in my sights. We were almost to the Cahuenga Pass when she whipped it around yet another bend. And came head on with an oncoming freighter.

Then it was nothing but blaring horns and bright lights.

CHAPTER THIRTY

TRUDY dug her dainty mitts into my arm. Buried her gorgeous map into my shoulder. I could barely stand to lamp the impending impact, either. If Irene didn't take him head on, she'd surely get airborne and launch over the cliff.

We both waited for the loud smash that was sure to follow. The sound of crumpling iron. And one or both crashing into the hungry belly of underbrush.

I slammed on the skids as the hulking lorry flew past. Horn blaring at maximum decibels.

Then it was silence. Dead silence.

Trudy was the first to speak up. "I didn't hear anything. Do you think she's all right?"

That's when I piped of a pair of tail lights up ahead. And saw them just as quickly disappear into the distance.

Lady Luck was with Irene. Because she'd somehow managed to pull it out and get around. Zipped straight across the Pass without a hitch.

"Yeah, I think she made it," I told her.

I slammed my dog on the pedal. Fed my crate another healthy shot of ethyl and rejoined the chase. Sniffed out the trail in no time. Managed to keep her in my sights well enough. Just when she'd drop out of sight, I'd catch her in my optics again, off in the distance.

Caught another glimpse as she turned onto Canyon Lake Road. If I'd known my way around a little better, I'd have realized: there was nowhere for her to go.

She was headed straight up into the Hollywood Hills. And would run out of road pretty quickly.

"Drats! We've lost her!" I shouted and banged my fisted duke on the dash. So hard I left a shallow crevice.

But once again, Trudy put her lovely, fact-filled noggin to good use. "No, we haven't," she informed me. "I know *exactly* where she's going."

CANYON LAKE took us around Lake Hollywood Park and onto Mulholland Highway. Which must've been somebody's idea of a joke, because it was anything but. Just another snaking, two-lane slab heading up the side of the peak.

Last turn was onto Mount Lee Drive, which quickly dissolved into just a dirt byway. Let me tell you, this one made Mulholland look like a straight shot.

It was a long, narrow artery with steep inclines and extra-wide turns. I was tempted to lay on the ethyl, but Trudy tipped me more than once: there was no need to hurry.

Next thing I knew, we'd reached the summit of Mount Lee. And a dead end to boot. Pulled to a stop right along the edge of the pavement.

At first glimpse, the only thing I saw was a large, two-story white edifice. Behind it stretched a 300-foot tower. At the time, the highest in the world.

Trudy explained that this was the Don Lee Studios, the first television broadcast studio in Los Angeles. They'd built on top of Mount Lee (named after said studio) to get the best signal. The place had everything: indoor and outdoor filming facilities, top-notch control room, and even a pool out back to televise bathing beauties.

Too bad they were closed up for the night.

And that's when it dawned on me. I knew *exactly* where we were. The most famous spot in all of LA. All I had to do was look *down* for a change.

HOLLYWOODLAND.

We'd parked just above the famous Sign.

Was sure different seeing it from the back. The whole caboodle was built on 24 giant telephone poles sunk into the ground, with a collection of wood scaffolding, pipes for wiring, and long beams to brace it against the ridge.

Each letter was about fifty foot tall, set another ten off the ground, and cut from sections of sheet metal. With a built-in ladder for changing the bulbs. All told, the whole thing stood a good sixty-foot high.

WE SPOTTED Irene's crate just a few yards off. She'd run it into the brush. Left the driver-side portal wide open.

Had to assume it was empty. But I was smart enough to be careful. This time.

I climbed out of my bucket and crouched down. Curiosity got the best of Trudy and she followed right behind me.

"Better stay behind the jalopy," I instructed. "And keep low."

Irene was one clever cupcake. Couldn't be too careful. No telling what tricks she *still* had up her sleeve.

I kept a solid optic on the tan coupe. Then I called out. "Irene?"

Dead quiet.

Went in for a closer look. Just as I thought. Vacant as a rectory on a Monday night.

Took a quick slant inside. Lamped a bit of blood on the wheel. She'd taken a bruiser after all.

The glovebox was open. Looked like she'd fished something out. A gat, maybe? It wouldn't take long to get my answer.

I stood up and piped around. The rain was still beating down like someone cut the faucet wide open. Felt like my pockets were filling with Adam's ale. Thunder cracked and rumbled overhead.

It was near pitch black out. Save for the moonlight and the city lights below. Then the occasional bolt of lightning that lit the hilltop up like the Chicago World's Fair.

Then I finally hung the focus on her.

Irene was just over the crest, headed towards the Sign. Doing her damndest to make it down the mountain. On foot.

But between the pitch blackness, the torrent of rain, and the muddy hillside, she hadn't gotten far.

Tough going. Especially for a dame. She shrieked in peak frustration.

I went to the edge and bellowed, "Irene! It's no use! You can't get away! You'll never make it!"

Wasn't sure she even heard me. She just kept struggling, trying to make it further down. But then she jerked back in my direction. Blood running down her beautiful forehead. Her optics blazing.

That's when I saw the roscoe in her grasp. And that she was ready to use it. "Oh, yeah? Just watch me!"

I called behind me, "Trudy! Get down!"

Irene spat lead in our direction. I dove for the pavement. And just in time.

Trudy screamed as all three shots whizzed past my cranium. Shattered the windows on my jalopy.

Yeah, she'd heard me alright. Loud and clear.

"Leave me alone!" Irene howled. Only she wasn't done. "I won't let them take me! I won't go to prison! I'm a star, do you hear me? A STAR!"

The she hosed two more slugs in our direction. And disappeared into the darkness below.

"Trudy, you okay?" I shouted.

"Yes! I think so!" she called back. Luckily, she'd stayed behind my crate. Otherwise she might've gotten a deadly dose of lead poisoning. Too many close calls with the Reaper in one night for my liking.

"Good!" I told her. "She's almost out."

"Oh, Tom! Please be careful!" Trudy begged.

"Don't worry," I did my best to assure her. Though I wasn't exactly convinced myself. "I'll be fine."

I surged to my brogans. Carefully made my way to the very edge of the hilltop. Thought I'd left the rainy nights and gunplay back in France. Only this time the enemy was blonde and shapely. And I was desperately short on ammo.

They say the pen is mightier than the sword. But it's got nothing against a gat. Especially when you're unarmed. By my count, she was down to one slug. I only hoped I was right.

But that was still enough to kill a man.

CHAPTER THIRTY-ONE

I KEPT LOW and crawled over the ledge. Made my way down to nab Irene. The rain was still coming down like the days of Noah. It was tough going, even for me.

Lightning flashed overhead and I lamped her again.

She'd slid down the muddy hillside. Skidded to a stop at the bottom of the the first L. She was already having a rough time of it. Getting down any further was going to be even harder. No way she'd make it the rest of the way unscathed.

Assuming that was her plan.

I did my best to talk her back. "Irene! I told you, there's nowhere for you to go! Give yourself up and maybe the cops will go easy on you!"

That's when she took one last shot at me. But this time she just fired off wildly into the night sky. Didn't hit a thing.

When she took another, she just pulled the trigger on an empty chamber. Over and over. And I huffed a sigh of relief.

Finally, she just bellowed out in frustration. Threw the gat into the ravine.

Trudy stayed huddled behind my jalopy. Made sure to keep 3000 lbs. of steel and iron between herself and Irene. Smart girl.

I called back to her. "It's okay, Trudy! Don't worry, she can't hurt me now."

Trudy was relieved, but still worried. "Oh, Tom! Do be careful!"

Finally had a minute to run the odds through my grey matter. And not worry about Irene filling me with daylight.

NO MORE deadly distractions. Only the rain pelting down and soaking us all clear to the bone.

Even if Irene did throw in the towel, there was no way she was climbing back up on her own. She was stuck down there, but good. And I wasn't about to just leave her there, either. Not in good conscience.

It all added up to only one choice. "Irene!" I barked. "That's it! I'm coming down to get you!"

I took one look back at Trudy and started my descent. Was even rougher than I expected. Only made it a few steps before I lost traction and took a good spill. Had to dig my mitts down into the mud to keep from sliding any further.

I'd gotten almost to the Sign when Irene voiced her displeasure. "Get away from me! I told you to get away!"

She threw her gaze in every direction. She was trapped and she knew it. Nothing stung worse than the wretched realization she'd soon get pinched.

The one thing she *hadn't* counted on.

She was out of options and she knew it. I'd seen enough men in her predicament to know: that's a lousy place to be. Like the baby-faced Nazi who unpinned a grenade just to take a few of us with him. And I'll never forget the look in his eye when he did it.

Never expected to see that look off the battlefield. Especially in a dame.

That's when she reared back up on her stems. Piped up at the giant L behind her. And grabbed a firm hold on the ladder.

It gave just a little, but otherwise held firm. When she was sure it wouldn't topple over just like the H, she clawed for a step just above her reach. And started to climb.

At first I couldn't believe my optics. *What did she think she was doing?*

That's when I realized I didn't want to know the answer. "Irene! Don't do this! You've got to come down!"

"No! Go away!" she howled back. "I'll *jump* before I go to prison!"

"I can't let you do this, Irene!" I countered. "It's not worth it!"

She had to be bluffing. She just *had* to!

She clawed up another couple of rungs. Hoisted herself up even higher. All to prove she meant business. "Don't come near me! I'll jump! I swear I'll jump!"

Trudy watched fearfully from the ledge. Lightning cracked again. Illuminated the whole mountaintop. If only for a second.

But all I could think about was Irene. Up there in that downpour. Clinging to the Sign.

I practically slid the rest of the way. Luckily, the L stopped me from pitching dome-first down the mountainside. I fixed a tight grip to keep from sprawling further.

"Don't move, Irene!" I reassured her. "I'm coming up!"

Trudy was practically beside herself, watching on pins and needles. "Tom, she's almost to the top!"

I did my best to reach up and grab her. A stem, a foot, anything. But she was already too high.

"Irene! Listen to me!" I barked. "If you don't come down, I'll climb up there and get you myself!"

Lightning flashed again as she just scaled higher.

Trudy shrieked, "Tom, you have to stop her!" This time I could barely hear.

That was it. Time to really put it in gear. "Okay, Irene! I'm coming up!"

I hustled as fast as I could. The rain was still beating down and the old ladder was slippery. But since Irene had a good head start, she still managed to beat me to the top.

Soon as I was within reach, she tried her best to kick me off. Even managed to get in a lick or two on my noggin with her heels. "Stop it! Leave me alone!"

I lost my grip and gravity got the best of me. Luckily, I only dropped a couple of rungs. Scraped up my paw pretty good. But sure beat hitting the ground.

Trudy could only watch from the summit. "Tom, be careful!"

Irene realized there was no stopping me. Made double

sure I knew she meant business. "Don't come any closer! I'll jump! I *swear* I'll jump!"

The sky lit up with a huge bolt of lightning. I knew the longer we were up there, the better the chance we both had of getting fried.

That was one thing I didn't think about. No matter which way this story ended, it was all she had to look forward to.

With me clambering my way back up, she crossed over to the O. I'll give her this. Can't say when I've ever seen a dame more determined.

I gave Kong a run for his money. Hustled it to the top of the L. Did my level best to grab her. But every time I reached out, she crawled further away. Just out of reach.

This time, though, I could glim her in the optics. Sure, she was facing a pretty long stretch. Maybe even the chair. But was this really how she wanted it to end? The coward's way out?

I begged her one last time. "Irene, please! You can't do this!"

That's when I saw it. The first and only time.

The real Irene.

No acting. No star power.

Just the God's honest truth. Straight from her cold, black heart.

Like so many other things in Hollywood. Beautiful and enticing on the outside. Dark and ugly on the inside.

Then she stood up on the scaffold.

Looked down into the shadow of the canyon below. Tears mixed with the rain.

And I realized there was just no stopping her.

"You don't understand," she confessed. "If I go to prison, they'll *forget* me."

Then she took one long, final gaze down into the void below.

"But if I jump, they'll remember me *forever!*"

CHAPTER THIRTY-TWO

I DID my best to catch her. I swear I did.

I'd like to think that I was only inches away. That the hem off her dress had just barely slipped through my fingers. But truth be told, I don't know how close I was.

I just know one thing.

I wasn't close enough.

When it was all over, there was nothing else I could do.

Except stare down into the blackness below. The blackness that had finally swallowed her up.

May God have mercy on her soul.

SOON as I clawed my way back up to the plateau, I found Trudy there waiting. She'd already banged on every door of the Studio. Either the joint was empty, or the night watchman was dead on his dogs.

We climbed back into my crate and made tracks for the nearest squawk box. By that time, the heavens had thankfully called off the waterworks. Took a moment to wring ourselves out. Gave her my jacket to keep warm. But it was like wiping up a ten-gallon spill with a wet dishrag.

Finally dropped a wet nickel and yodeled Underwood. Told him to meet me at the office. Told him it was urgent. When he squirmed for details, I proclaimed I'd broken the entire arson case. Can't be sure, but I think he actually hung up first.

Then I rang the boss and told him to hold the front page.

He was ready to throw me out on my ear. Naturally, the cops'd already been to the Saltzman blaze in Beverly Hills. Jenkins had tried to yodel me all night. And was rightfully spitting nails again when he couldn't get through.

Once I'd already gotten an earful, I barked in opposition. "Can it, Jenkins! I've got the whole scoop! I was *inside* that tinder box when it went up!"

For a second I thought the line went dead.

Jenkins didn't make a peep. Not until he'd picked his jaw up off the floor.

"You what?" he finally inquired. "Then why didn't you stick around? Or phone it in? Just where in the Sam Hill have you been?"

"You better sit down for this one," I alerted him. "I was with Irene Faye when she *jumped* off the Hollywoodland Sign!"

JENKINS WAS still swooning when we trotted into the City Room. And even though we didn't spare the horsepower, Underwood was already there waiting for us.

Trudy and I were both still soaked to the bone. And she was shivering like a newborn Eskimo. So Gronchi rounded up a couple of blankets and a fresh pot of java. Yeah, I was surprised, too.

Anyways, that's when I laid out the whole thing. Every last detail. About Irene. Kellman. The fake Saltzman. The fires. Everything. Even told Underwood where they could find the corpse.

Of course, Gronchi couldn't help but shake her dainty noggin. And harrumph when I explained how Trudy'd spoiled Irene's dastardly plan.

"Maybe we should put *her* on the payroll," she commented.

Jenkins and Underwood just shook their domes in disbelief. Especially about Kellman. I wasn't the only one chasing that boogeyman. But Trudy was there to back me up. On every word.

And once the cops finally nabbed the Fake Saltzman, he did just the same. All they had to do was name him as an accomplice. Then he sang like a canary. Anything to keep his own keister out of the slammer. And get his mug on the front page.

Once I'd finished jawing, Jenkins kicked into high gear. He grabbed the nearest horn and started barking orders. First to the press room. Then a team of copy men. All of whom had to call their wives to say they wouldn't make it home before daylight.

By the time Underwood left, it was getting pretty late. Too late to take Trudy home, anyways. She wasn't that keen on it, either.

I'd thought about the Strand hotel up the street. But as usual, Gronchi beat me to it. She had Trudy bunk in an empty office. We kept it furnished with a spare cot, pillow, and blankets for just such an occasion.

Jenkins had put it to good use himself many times. And would've done the same that night if it wasn't already taken.

CHAPTER THIRTY-THREE

SOON as the early morning sun hit the southern slope of Mount Lee, Underwood had a couple dozen harness bulls scour the underbrush. The morning edition was just hitting the streets. Coppers were itching to find the body. Especially before the hillside was filled peak to valley with lookie-loos.

My pal Rigby, the young rookie who'd let me in the file room, was first to spot her. He caught a glimpse of her golden blonde tresses tangled in the thicket.

Poor kid. It was a sight he wouldn't soon forget.

Me, either. And I'd seen a lot worse on the battlefield duking it out with the Nazis.

She was in a crumpled heap near the bottom of the ravine. Hair and torso caked in mud. Hard to tell just what was dried earth and what was blood. Neck and limbs pointing off in impossible directions.

The crime scene camera boy burned off a roll in less than a minute. While we just stood there and lamped in any other direction.

Hands down the worst pictures Irene ever took.

But not the one for which she'd be remembered. Before the ink was dry on the morning edition, the Studio swooped in like a pack of wolves. Same studio that wouldn't touch her only a day earlier.

Took control of the story. All under the direction of the

Real Derek. With that bulldog of a fixer, Eddie Lennox, leading the charge. Made sure every paper, the *Chronicle* included, had the best 8x10 glossies.

Irene at her most beautiful.

That's the way I wanted to remember her, too. Not the way she looked crumpled up at the bottom of that mountain. Or even just a few hours earlier, dangling atop the Sign that presently loomed over us.

No time at all before the crime scene was lousy with camera boys and the rest of the newshounds in town. All hot on the trail. Eager to get whatever scoop they could.

Was on my way out when I ran into a familiar pair of stems. As I expected, the view led up to a beautiful map. Crowned with a silky coiffure of midnight tresses.

"What's the rush, Flyboy?" she queried. "Coppers making you nervous?"

"Got all I came to see, Doll," I informed her. "Might want to steer clear. Not a pretty sight for a lady."

"I see one, I'll be sure to warn her," she smirked, then tossed a nod in Irene's direction. "Looks like you beat me to the punch after all. Didn't think you had it in you."

If I hadn't known any better, I'd have thought she'd just paid me a compliment. Certainly as close as I'd get to one. "Or maybe I just got lucky," I replied. Which was closer to the truth than I'd ever admit.

"Maybe," she added. Though if I didn't know any better, the smirk that followed could've been mistaken for a grin.

Was just about to make tracks when she stopped me again. Something had gotten under her beautiful, soft skin. And it was bugging her something fierce. "Tell me something, since you've got all the answers."

She locked lamps on me to see if I would powder. I didn't.

"So Irene Faye's house burns down last night," she reasoned, "and from what I hear, nearly with you and your little sweetheart in it."

"That's right," I confirmed. No sense in holding back. That much was already in the history books. Plastered all over the morning edition.

She moved in close to get my attention. In spades, to boot. "Then she goes and offs herself by jumping off the

Hollywoodland Sign. And once again, *you're* right there in the thick of it. You got the *inside scoop*. Front page. All over town."

That jane sure knew how to work a room. But by that time, I was getting impatient. "What're you getting at, Doll? Go ahead, spill it. Or get lost."

"Sure she wasn't *pushed*?" she queried.

If she wasn't a dame, I'd have sent her on a trip to the carpet right there. Launched my dukes right in her kisser. Don't believe I didn't think twice about it.

"Yeah, I'm sure," I growled. "I got a witness."

"Right, your little *sweetheart*."

I didn't like the inference. It was one thing to take a swipe at me. I could take it. Especially from her dainty mitts. But Trudy was off limits.

Before I could object further, she was at me with another query. "Just one more thing. Tell me, just how does any of this square with Kellman and the arson case?"

I just looked at her and shook my cranium. Wasn't about to make it that easy.

"Forget it, Doll. You're just going to have to read about it in the morning edition. Like everybody else."

WHEN I got back to the *Chronicle*, first thing I did was drop in on Trudy. She was still holed up in the spare hovel. She'd looked like Sleeping Beauty when I left her. And then some. I wanted to do my best Prince Charming when I darkened her gate. Kneel right down and wake her with a kiss.

Instead I found her sitting up, wide awake. Already back from dreamland. Sipping a cup of joe and chin wagging with Gronchi. That had me more anxious than my run-in with Flora Mason.

I gave a little knock on the portal. "Morning, Angel. Sleep okay?"

She stifled a dainty yawn, nodded in affirmation. "Oh, Tom! Thank goodness you're back. I was just asking Janet where you were. Is everything okay?

Janet? Who's Janet? Took me a second to connect the wires. Before I realized she was referring to Gronchi.

"Yeah," I told her. "Just had to step out for a few. Tie up some loose ends."

Gronchi gave me a nod. Think it might've even been approval. Though I couldn't imagine I'd actually done something right. First Flora Mason, now the Italian spitfire. Was expecting a call from my mother at any moment, congratulating me on a job well done.

"You hungry?" I asked. "There's a hash house just around the corner. Figured we could grab a booth and snag a bite. I have to square things with the boss, first."

"That would be just wonderful, thank you," she yawned again. "I just need to run to the powder room and freshen up."

Gronchi pointed her in the right direction. Then stopped me on the way out. The twisted look on her map was more to my expectation. "You were right. I *do* like this gal. Which is why she's too good for you."

For once, I had to agree.

ON OUR way out, I led Trudy back down to the City Room. Place was just as we'd left it. Filled to the brim with the sound of clacking typewriters, chattering copy editors, and my fellow newshounds preaching the latest scoop. All of whom stunk of day-old coffee, empty liquor bottles, and burnt-out gaspers.

Lording over it all was Jenkins. Barking back and forth. Beaming ear-to-ear. Waving the morning edition like another prize trophy.

"MOVIE STAR JUMPS TO DEATH FROM HOLLYWOODLAND SIGN!" he shouted. "Now that's a banner headline if I ever saw one!"

The boss grabbed me by the mitt, gave me a firm handshake. A welcome change from chewing out my keister just a day earlier.

"Great work, Miller! Between this and wrapping up the arson story, you've got enough headlines to carry us for a week!"

"Thanks, Mr. Jenkins," I did my best to muster the appropriate level of gratitude. But it would be a long time before I could shake the guilt. If only I'd been just a little quicker. "Believe me, I tried to save her. I really did —"

Jenkins was just as quick with the consolation. "Don't worry, Son. You did the best you could."

Trudy did him a few times better. She wrapped her slender wings around me. "Tom, I'm so sorry. But I'm just glad you're okay! I love you! I really love you!"

"Yeah, me too, kid," I replied. Like I said before. I was falling hard for this doll. There was just no denying it.

Jenkins wasn't through, though, and gave me a hearty pat on the back. "You've done a man's job, Miller. Why don't you take the day off? Take this gal to a movie or something. You've earned it."

"Sure thing, Mr. Jenkins," I told him. "Thanks. But I think we've both had enough of the picture business for a while."

Trudy was in full agreement. "I think I'd settle for a nice, quiet evening at home."

"You said it, Angel."

That was our happy ending. For the time being anyways.

Little did I know there was an arrest warrant waiting just around the corner.

And with Trudy's name on it.

But happiness is like anything else in Hollywood.

It can never last too long.

END.

BONUS:
THE RED-HEADED RUSE

I AIMED my bucket with all horses blazing towards NBC Radio at the corner of Sunset and Vine. Didn't let off the ethyl until I slammed to a stop. The skid was heard two blocks away. No worries about the cops, though. Because Lt. Hap Underwood, my well-dressed compadre at the L.A.P.D, burned to a stop right behind me.

"Breck call you, too?" I queried.

"Of course," Underwood chuckled as he slid out of his police-issue coupe. "This is a legal matter, too, you know."

We breezed in through the double glass doors. Tossed a quick wave to the cute little blonde jane behind the desk. Under other circumstances, I wouldn't have minded waiting.

But this wasn't other circumstances. No need for protocol.

The middle-aged, horn-rimmed station manager, Herman Breck, was already waiting for us. Puzzled expression and all.

"So, what's this unbelievable scoop?" I asked him.

He sucked in a quick breath. Then exhaled: "I've got the 'monkey wrench' back in my office. Wants to go on the radio and tell his side of the story."

Underwood and I both did a double-take on that one.

"When did he get here?" I asked.

Hap, being the laid-back type, was more than willing to let me take the lead. He knew I would anyway.

"'Bout an hour ago. Seems he hitched his way down from Fort Lewis, up in Washington."

FIRST THING I learned in the newspaper game was you never know which way a story's gonna go. Sometimes, you think you've got it all figured out. Then it takes a wild turn from out of nowhere. And sometimes that wild turn goes bust. And you're right back where you started.

My fellow newshounds and I had all been chasing the latest Carmine Calvero story for weeks on end. As you know, Calvero was world famous for his "Lucky Hobo" character back in the silent days.

Of course, he'd long put away the grease-paint and baggy pants. But that didn't stop him from enjoying his remaining star power.

One of his latest conquests was a fiery, red-haired dish named Joanne Benton. They had some laughs. Then he sent her packing, just like all the others.

Only this one showed up on his doorstep some months later. Mad as hell, and with a bundle of joy to boot. Not to mention a lawyer.

The "monkey wrench" came in the form of a telegram from a Chaplain up in Washington State. Sent to a judge in Beverly Hills: "Soldier here admits intimacy with Joanne Benton. Believes he is the father."

Needless to say, this bit of news hit like a thunder storm at a Sunday picnic. Lawyers on both sides went scrambling. One side hoped it was true. The other hoped it wasn't. I'm sure Calvero got at least one night's good sleep from it.

With company, no doubt.

BRECK SPILLED the whole scenario on the way down the hall. "Kid's name is Fred Steinman. Fresh-faced private in Uncle Sam's Army. Says he was stationed for a while down here last year. Picked her up in his jeep one night and took her up into the Hollywood hills. The view sent her swooning so hard, she jumped right into his loving arms."

Underwood popped the question we were both asking:

"So, you think this kid's legit?"

"Talks a good game to me," Breck shrugged. "But what do I know?"

"Sounds fishy to me," I offered. "If he's for real, why go on the radio? Why not just go straight to see the gal?"

Hap nodded in agreement. "So, what're you thinking?"

"I say we put him to the test."

"How so?" Breck asked.

"He wants to talk to the press. But he'll clam when he sees Hap's badge. So, we tell him Hap's the Benton quail's brother. Then we see what shakes out."

Hap shook his head in disagreement. "I'm a cop, not an actor."

"Alright then," I countered. "You be me and I'll be the brother. Just let me ask all the questions."

We all nodded in agreement. Breck took us back to his office where the kid was stewing.

MY GLIMS lit up like search lights on Hollywood Boulevard when Fred stood up to greet us. His shadow could cover Mt. Rushmore. He had me by nearly a foot. And I'm a full two yards in my bare feet.

"When do I go on the radio?" the young private asked. He clutched his green army cap in frustration. "When can I see Joanne?"

"In time," Breck told him calmly. "But first I want you to meet some people. This is Tom... Benton, Joanne's brother."

I stuck out my mitt. His paw swallowed mine like a vise.

I suddenly got worried about the ruse we were playing. Or what he'd do when he found out the truth.

"And," Breck continued and pointed out Hap. This is uh... Tom Miller, with the *L.A. Chronicle*."

Breck wasn't too good himself with play-acting, either. Of course, a few seconds deciding on names wouldn't have hurt.

Fred gave us both a curious grin. "Both named Tom, huh?"

Not wanting to blow the ruse right out of the gate, I jumped in. Went right to brass tacks.

"Why do you want to marry my sister?" I asked.

"Because I love her," the hulking lug swooned. "I didn't know she was — you know, in the family way 'till I read about it in the papers. Honest, I didn't! I just felt terrible. I'm not the kind of fellah who'd run out on a gal like that! I want to do right by her. Take care of her. I love her more than any woman in the world."

"So, what's your plan?" I asked him.

"I'm gonna ask her to marry me. With your permission, of course." He fumbled in his pocket. Pulled out a small ring with a tiny speck for a stone. "I'll be out of the service, soon. I've already arranged with my sister in Jersey for us to stay with her 'till we can get a place of our own."

If nothing else, the kid was sincere.

If it was an act, it was an awful good one. And he was in just the right town for it.

Hap gave me a heartfelt look. "How about it, Tom?"

"Okay," I told him. "You can meet her for dinner on one condition: *Don't* go on the radio."

The buck private's map lit up. He jumped to his pins. Shook my duke like a dirty rug. "Sure thing, Mr. Benton! You have my word!"

Hap and Breck saved their questions until we'd left the office. Well out of earshot.

"How do you plan to get this kid together with Joanne Benton?" Hap asked.

Breck pointed out the more obvious hurdle. "She's in the funny farm!"

"Simple," I told them. "We hire a ringer."

ONE MORE thing the kid didn't know: After she'd shown up at Calvero's palace with baby in tow, the aging funny man had refused to see her. So, she came back after dark and forced her way in. More than once.

That'd earned her a one-way ticket to the hospital. The psychiatric kind. And managed to slow her down a bit.

But not her lawyer. He'd managed to chock it up to "emotional duress." All caused by Calvero, of course.

After we parted ways at the station, I hopped back in my jalopy. Took the five-minute drive over to Central Casting in the Mayer Bldg. at Hollywood and Western.

THE RED-HEADED RUSE

I'd been there enough that I no longer had to show my credentials. Betty Marsden was the smart-looking blonde jane who usually worked the counter. Her smile lit up the room when I walked in. I always wondered what she was doing *behind* it.

"Hey, Winchell," she asked. "What're you up to this time?" She knew any day I ankled my way into her portal, it would get interesting.

"Need a gal that can pass for Joanne Benton. There's two sawbucks in it for her if she plays along."

Betty dipped her cheaters and raised an eyebrow.

"Don't worry, Doll. It's strictly on the level. Just a night out for dinner, that's all."

She knew better than to ask any more questions. "You're in luck. I've got just the girl."

She went through the filing cabinet. Whisked through a drawer of glossies.

Seconds later, she plopped one in front of my puss. "Her name's Louise Gribble. Ever since the Benton story broke, people are always saying how much Louise looks like her."

She was right. The gal bore a striking resemblance.

Since I was gambling that Fred had only seen the real Joanne in newsprint, she'd do perfectly. Either way, it would still prove my point.

"Tell her to meet me at the Formosa, Five Forty-Five, sharp."

YOUNG MISS GRIBBLE must have been hungry for work. Or just plain hungry. Because she was early.

I was glad, too, because it gave us a few minutes to prepare. I tabbed her as soon as her long stems stepped off the Red Car. Her fiery red hair framed a face that looked even better in Technicolor.

I rushed over and scooped her up by the arm. "Louise Gribble?"

Soon as she answered in the affirmative, I whisked her in through the front canopy. "I'm Tom Miller with the *L.A. Chronicle*."

Then I proceeded to feed her the run-down on our little game. After I'd spilled the details, she was still willing to play along.

There was just one problem. Two, actually.

Everyone knows Calvero was drawn to Joanne Benton's ample charms. But for all her other delectable attributes, this wren was built like an ironing board.

I gave her the up-and-down once more. "Look, Sweetheart, you're perfect. But we've got to make an adjustment."

"Sure you're a reporter? Or a *producer*?" She shot back with a smile that made my knees give.

She was as sharp as she looked. I liked that.

Her dark skirt and auburn tresses were a perfect match for the Formosa's red-and-black décor. The walls are topped with signed photos of every famous mug in Tinsel Town. Her face could have fit with any one of them.

I breezed her over to the hostess stand. Luckily, the lovely brunette quail was eager to assist.

"Listen, Sweetheart, I need a box of tissues, pronto." I dropped a few bills to show I was in a hurry.

Another glance at Louise and I decided to up the order. "Make it two."

The hostess cutie got my message. She replaced my bills with two boxes in seconds flat. I pushed them into Louise's dainty mitts.

"No offense, Sweetheart. But we need to fill you out a little. Meet me in the dining car when you're ready."

She got the gist and smiled back. "Of course. I'll just be in the powder room."

I tabbed Jim Perry, staff photog, ready and waiting.

If Fred turned out to be the real deal, he'd be on the front page of the morning edition. If not, we didn't know what he'd do when he found out we were wise to him.

Hap was armed, just in case. That's why we'd come there early. Just so there wouldn't be any innocent bystanders.

"Right this way, Sir," the hostess cutie chirped as she led me past the bar towards the "dining car" in the back — a retired trolley from the Red Car line. The rest of the joint was built around it.

Miss Gribble returned a few minutes later. She looked like a different girl and completely natural. They certainly got my attention. And I knew better.

THE RED-HEADED RUSE

Just in time, too. Because seconds later, Hap and Breck strolled in with our young quarry.

"Joanne!" he called out as soon as he lamped her. He reached out for a hug, but she ducked behind my back. His towering size took her by surprise, too.

"Hello, Joanne darling," he pined, "it's so good to see you again."

She eyed him nervously.

"Hello, Fred," she replied. "It's lovely to see you again, too."

Her radiant smile calmed him down. He took her hand and went to kiss it. Then chickened out — out of shyness.

That led to a few long seconds of awkward silence.

So, I jumped in to break the ice. "What do you say we get a picture of you two lovebirds together?"

But my true aim was for Fred to get a *really* good look at "Joanne." And see which way the dominoes fell.

The "happy family" posed while photog Perry snapped a few plates. Fred was still none the wiser.

Which was all I needed to see. I gave Hap the nod and tapped Fred on the shoulder.

"Fred, let's go outside a minute. I need to ask you something. Man to man."

Fred gave me a big, goofy grin. "Sure thing, Mr. Benton."

"Breck, you mind staying with Joanne?" I asked. I could tell from the goofy smirk on his own mug that he didn't.

We ankled it back out the front portico. I peered back to make sure Hap was right behind me.

SOON AS we got outside, I put it to the young private. "What do you want to lie for, Fred?" I asked. "You've never seen this doll before in your life."

Fred just turned red-faced and shrugged, "Wh-why would I lie?"

"That's what we want to know," I barked.

Hap brushed back his coat. Revealed his tin.

"This is serious business, kid," he said. "Could land you in a lot of hot water."

Fred dug in his heels like a bull about to charge.

"What are you trying to pull on me here?" he demanded.

He just barreled straight past us. Right back inside.

That got us even more scared.

Hap grabbed for his roscoe as we followed suit. Hell bent for leather.

WHEN WE got to the dining car, poor Breck was the only thing between Fred and Louise. I don't know who was more frightened — him or the girl.

Photog Perry was dutifully grabbing shots. Ready to capture the moment of Breck getting pummeled.

"You know it's true, don't you honey? Tell 'em! Tell 'em how we loved each other that night in the hills!"

He reached for her with his big paws. But she jerked loose. Ducked behind Hap and his iron equalizer.

"Get away from me, you big goof! I'm not Joanne Benton and I never was in the hills with you!"

Fred just stood there. Dumb expression on his map. He'd been had, but good.

"What are you trying to do? Mix me up?" he shouted back. He was starting to get flustered.

"Ix-nay, Fred," I told him. "Get yourself together. You've been putting on a good act. But the show's over."

Fred boiled up like a volcano. Hap had his bean-shooter cranked and ready.

Fred just growled like he was going to pop. Then he bolted straight out the front door.

We followed after. Just in time to see him haul it on foot down Santa Monica Boulevard.

We'd hoped that was the last we'd ever see of one Private Fred Steinman.

I gave our "Joanne," the now less vivacious (but still quite lovely) Louise Gribble, an extra ten-spot when I escorted her back to the Red Car.

"Thanks, Doll, and sorry about all the drama."

"I think next time I'll just stick to work in *front* of the camera," she told me.

I couldn't blame her.

THREE DAYS passed, and there was no sign of Private Fred.

THE RED-HEADED RUSE

I figured he must have found his way back to Washington State. Given up on his dreams of rescuing red-headed damsels.

I figured wrong.

I came into the office early one morning. Plopped down at my desk to fuss over another angle on the Calvero story. That's when I heard a familiar voice in the doorway.

"I need to talk to a reporter. I got a *real* scoop for you. On the Joanne Benton story."

I peered up from my typewriter to see young Fred. He was towering over the desk of stone-gazed Janet Gronchi, our no-nonsense Gal Friday.

I always said she'd be a real cutie if she'd let down her hair and perked up her disposition. But this was not the day.

Fred had regrouped. Now he was angling for the papers. "I need to talk to someone right away! I tell you, it's important!" He barked. Big mistake.

That was enough to get the attention of our seen-it-all City Editor Hal Jenkins, sitting in his office. He glanced up from his desk, peered out the large windows. Took in the sight of the big palooka looming over our tiny damsel.

Now, Jenkins could have jumped in. But he knew it wasn't necessary.

Gronchi rose up out of her chair. Grabbed her quarter-inch thick wooden ruler. Stared Fred down through her horn-rimmed cheaters. No easy feat, as he was more than twice her height.

But there's not a man nor beast alive that can out-intimidate Gronchi.

She stuck her ruler right in his face. "You'll talk to someone when I tell you to. And not a minute sooner! You got that?"

"Yes, Ma'am," Fred backed off, tail between his legs.

"Now sit down!"

"It's okay, Gronchi," I piped up. "I'll jaw with him."

Soon as Fred's optics locked on mine, I could see the light bulb blink on over his head.

That's when he finally realized that I wasn't "Joanne's" brother. That he'd really been had. *Completely*.

The volcano was about to blow for real this time.

Of course, it might have been smarter to let Fred tangle with Gronchi. But I was wise enough to ask for back-up.

"Better call Hap, Gronchi! Tell him the Private's back!" I shouted.

I don't know who was faster: Gronchi spinning the phone dial, or Fred flying across the desks towards me. Papers and typewriters chucking in all directions.

I shoved my desk forward. Caught him in the shins. Just enough to slow him down!

But not by much.

Jenkins shouted from his office, "What the hell?"

Then he ordered Gronchi to find photog Perry.

A newsman to the bone. If I was going to die, he wanted it on film.

Fred's giant fists came at me like two anvils shot out of a cannon.

My plan was simple. Keep away from those dukes!

I usually rely on my own bulk in fights. But not this time. I was the one who had to be quicker.

Fred swung his left, then his right! Came up empty both times. The desk had done its job. He was big and sloppy. Just as I suspected.

I ducked on the third, but wasn't so lucky then. Hit my chin like a freight train!

Sent me reeling into the wall! Never had a wallop like that before. Wasn't sure what was spinning faster: me or the room!

Caught a quick glimpse of Gronchi shouting into the squawker.

But Fred was back for seconds.

Despite my dizziness, I managed to avoid the return of the Steinman Express. Fred hit the wall instead. I swear it shook the building!

Needed to clear my head. And *something* to even the odds. Jenkins was already on it. Kept a Louiseville Slugger in his office for just such an occasion.

Fred came at me again. I lunged to avoid his next swing.

THE RED-HEADED RUSE

Jenkins threw me the bat.

I didn't waste any time. Needed to make it good!

Went for the kneecap with everything I had. Managed to get a wince. But it wasn't enough!

Next I aimed high.

Big mistake! Fred was quicker than I thought.

Caught the bat in his right hand! Caught my chin again with his left!

Thought it would shatter! Sent me sprawling back towards Gronchi's desk.

Left me seeing double. Tried to stagger to my feet.

Fred had the upper hand. And the bat! Hap couldn't get there soon enough.

I looked around.

Stab him with a pencil? Hit him with a stapler?

The bat was my best weapon. And now *he* had it!

And he was about to use it. On me!

Fred raised up the bat. Was just about to bring it crushing down on my skull!

That's when the cavalry showed up.

"Hey!" Gronchi shouted. "Didn't I tell you to sit down?"

My optics widened. So, did Fred's.

Jenkins wasn't the least surprised.

Gronchi marched up to Fred. Stuck her thick ruler right up in his map.

"You put that bat down right now, Mister!"

Fred's button went blank. The color ran right out.

"Y-yes, Ma'am," he stuttered. Dropped the slugger just like he was ordered.

"Now you help clean this mess up, and I mean *NOW*!"

That was all the opening I needed. I balled up my dukes. Let him have it with every ounce of juice I had left!

Right in the smeller! The little crack told me I'd hit pay dirt.

Yeah, it was a sucker punch.

But I owed him one for tossing me around the room like a rag doll.

"Who is this clown?" Gronchi asked. Fred's sniffer oozed like a faucet with a really bad leak.

"Just a guy who tried to sell a bad story one too many times," I shot back.

HAP SHOWED up not too long after with a couple of harness bulls. Plus an Army Lieutenant and a pair of MPs.

Just in time to see Gronchi riding herd over Private Fred with tissues stuffed up each nostril.

She tapped her ruler impatiently as every desk, every typewriter, and every paper was put back in its place.

Jenkins was already back in his office. He knew better than to get in the way.

"You boys can sit right over there and wait," Gronchi piped. She pointed to a row of chairs with her ruler. "You can have him when I'm done. And not a minute *sooner*."

"Yes, Ma'am," the Lieutenant replied.

Perry snapped another photograph.

END.

WHAT HAPPENED TO TRUDY?

Tear-stained eyes and a torn blouse are pretty strong clues that Trudy's screen test didn't go as she'd hoped. Find out just what happened in our companion tale, DREAMS DIE AT SUNSET. In Trudy's own words.
bit.ly/dreamsdie

Get your FREE copy today when you join THE BLACK SPECTRE COVERT LEAGUE.

And that's not all! You'll also receive the latest news from Black Hood Press, more freebies, and other member exclusives. We promise to never spam you. Because spamming is evil, and we are here to fight evil.

www.blackhoodpress.com

READ THE FIRST EXCITING CHAPTER!

An ambitious reporter looking for her big break.
A millionaire recluse looking for a cure.
Can they survive a violent, corrupt city?

Vicky Rose is a reporter stuck in the City Hall beat, but she knows she's destined to cover crime. She sees her chance at a big break when the mayor is murdered in his office.

Reclusive millionaire Brent Gregor has been trapped in a wheelchair since the night a home intruder killed his father. Now, the only thing he cares about is being able to walk again.

The mayor's murder reeks of mob violence, but all the evidence points to someone else. Vicky knows the only hope of finding the truth rests in Gregor's hands, but he's unwilling to help until the one person who might be able to cure him changes his mind….

www.blackhoodpress.com

About the Author

Roger Alford grew up on a steady diet of *Star Wars* and Jim Henson. After discovering old time radio and movie serials in college, he realized he'd been born in the wrong decade. His Internet videos, which include the popular mash-ups *The Twilight Zone: Planet of the Apes* and *Raiders of the Lost Ark: The Serial*, have been featured on ABC News, CNN, Inside Edition, plus multiple books and newspapers. When he's not plotting the latest adventures of The Black Spectre or brushing up on Mafia history, he's traveling the country and eating in great restaurants with his wife and family.

INDIA:
18-22-15-16-20 3-26-14 26 6-15-5 14-3-17-18

www.ingramcontent.com/pod-product-compliance
Lightning Source LLC
Chambersburg PA
CBHW031445040426
42444CB00007B/979